SUPERPLONK

Malcolm Gluck writes the 'Superplonk' column in the *Weekend Guardian*. He is also wine correspondent of *City Limits* magazine and broadcasts wine phone-ins on LBC.

SUPERPLONK
Gluck's Guide to Supermarket Wine

Malcolm Gluck

faber and faber
LONDON · BOSTON

First published in 1991
by Faber and Faber Limited
3 Queen Square London WC1N 3AU
Reprinted in 1991
This new edition first published in 1991

Photoset by Parker Typesetting Service Leicester
Printed in England by Clays Ltd St Ives plc

© Malcolm Gluck, 1991

The author acknowledges with thanks permission to quote from *The
Penguin Book of Wines* by Allan Sichel (Penguin Books, revised 2nd edition
1971), © The Estate of Allan Sichel, 1965, © Revision, Peter A. Sichel,
1971.

Malcolm Gluck is hereby identified as author of this work in accordance
with Section 77 of the Copyright, Designs and Patents Act 1988

A CIP record for this book is available from the British Library

ISBN 0-571-16578-8

To Sue,
who always said we should have
a second one

Contents

Introduction

When I wrote *Superplonk*, my first guide to supermarket wine, last year, I believed I was approaching everything from a viewpoint of ruthless objectivity. I was, I thought, an open-minded bloke, free from prejudice. Well, it isn't so. I realized this when I read the first review of the *Guide*, by Cyril Ray in the *Guardian* newspaper. 'It is the merit of Malcolm Gluck's book,' Mr Ray wrote, 'that, in the spirit of the American sage who opined that "what this country needs is a good five-cent cigar", he acts upon the principle that what *this* country needs is a drinkable bottle of wine at three quid or less.' Mr Ray smote the nail unerringly on the head. There is simply no escaping the charge that I start from a prejudiced position. I want wine to be cheap. I also want it to be good; if possible, very good. Good grief, I am riddled with prejudice! The question is: does it matter? And, if it does, is this a good or a bad thing? It does matter, of course, if my bias renders me incapable of judging the true merits of expensive wines: it is, then, a bad thing. But I write and judge wines for my readers as much as for myself. And these readers, I hope, feel as I do. Good wine does not have to be expensive but expensive wine *has* to be good. The fact is that pricey bottles are often duff. I sometimes taste wines costing £15, £20, and £25 a bottle and wonder how the perpetrators of such crimes get away with it. But it seems that there will always be people who will judge a wine by its name, by its region and by its fancy price tag and by the effect such pretensions have on their friends; they cannot, it seems, judge a wine by the effect it has on their senses. This book has not been written for such credulous folk.

For non-readers like these, wine is not a pleasure for the eye, the nose or the mouth. It is an object of veneration – to be collected and flaunted, perhaps, like art or jewellery – not a principle of everyday enjoyment. I can do no better, in this respect, than to quote the late great Allan Sichel. In his *Penguin Book of Wines*, published in 1965, he took up his sharp quill pen and stuck it firmly in the rump of such pretensions.

Wine-drinking is no occult art to be practised only by the gifted few. Indeed, it is not an art at all. It is, or should be, the sober habit of every normal man and woman burdened with normal reponsibilities and with a normal desire to keep their problems in perspective and themselves in good health. It is meant for those who have the courage to enjoy the rhythm of life, not for those whose pleasure lies in exaggerating its miseries. Neither is it a panacea, meant to kill pain by dulling the sensibilities; it is a food for the body and mind from which a human being can draw the strength that will enable him to use to the full any gifts with which Nature has endowed him. It changes no one; it will not turn a creative artist into a scientist, a musician into a painter or a poet into a businessman. It will enrich each. It can be beneficial to everyone and enjoyed in varying degrees according to individual pockets and palates.

Pockets and palates; how often does the depth of one match the shallowness of the other? It is my fervent hope that this *Guide* will introduce increasing numbers of people to the idea that you do not need to be well-heeled to indulge regularly in drinkable wines, or even remotely wealthy to relish exciting ones. Who needs to spend £20 on a dodgy white burgundy when for one-sixth of this amount clean, fruity and infinitely better adjusted wines are available at supermarkets? As you buy your washing powder and baked beans so can you acquire outstanding wines. Think of this book as a map leading to a myriad of such treasures and a guide to many resultant pleasures.

Quite immodestly, it seems to me an extremely timely publication. We need to know where the bargain wines are to be found. For not only has wine consumption in this country declined for the first time in donkey's years, in part due to a series of immoderate price rises during '89 and '90 when the country was in a state of severe economic depression, but the 1991 budget increase of 9.3 per cent in duty, increasing the cost of wine from 9p to 18p depending on alcoholic strength, and the upping of VAT to 17.5 per cent, placed further crippling disincentives in the way of the wine-lover. (When will Chancellors of the Exchequer ever learn? As long ago as 1824 wine-lover James Warre persuasively argued the case against tax hikes on wine in a book with the catchy title *The Past, Present and Probably the Future State of the Wine Trade*. The subtitle was 'How every increase in duty leads to a decrease in income and a decrease in duty leads to an increase in income'.)

Certainly the 1991 budget finally laid on the doorstep of history the £1.99 bottle of wine. It barely survived the Chancellor's shenanigans in 1990, of course, but there were odd bottles under £2 to be found in supermarkets, although it must be admitted that these were usually special offers for a limited period only. Scandalously, in 1990, the Exchequer made over seven times more from a bottle of wine costing £1.99 than did its maker. Excise duty stood at 77p, bottling and freightage accounted for around 35p, and for the cost of retailing, including the profit to the store, 50p. Value Added Tax, a curious titular anomaly as it adds no value whatsoever, merely soaking the ultimate consumer, put on another 15 per cent. To the wine grower barely 10p. Ten pence!

From the point of view of this *Guide*, which takes into consideration the price of a wine in arriving at its points rating, this is very frustrating. Wines which were marvellous bargains a year or so back at between £1.99 and £2.75 ended up, over a matter of months, costing anything from £2.35 to £3.45. And now, of course, after the appalling thuggery of the 1991 budget, robbing the wine drinker to fob off the poll tax payer, things are even worse. Excise duty is so high it's extortion and VAT is so crippling it's sheer piracy.

Thus Mr Ray's observation at the beginning of this introduction, that I operate on the principle that what this country needs is a good bottle of wine at £3 or less is, alas, on the road to obsolescence. There are good bottles to be found at that price, but increasingly the £4 barrier – unthinkable twenty-four months ago – lurks just around the corner. This is, of course, for ordinary table wines. Champagne signalled its cynical and venal decision to go higher and higher without oxygen some time ago so that it could contrive to sit itself alongside caviare and truffles as an unobtainable item except to the super-rich or the temporarily insane. As you will discover as you go through the *Guide*, this wine, with the exception of the odd bottle, is now hardly worth recommending, since sparkling wines from the north, the middle and the south of France, the north of Italy and the south of Australia are proving much better value for money and, in some instances, more complex and rewarding tipples to boot. Champagne is betting, not unreasonably, on its entrenched position as a wine *par excellence*, a wine without real perceived rivals, to maintain its place in drinkers' affections and thus to have first call on their pockets when the real thing is required. Increasingly, however, the real thing is indifferently made, insufficiently aged and of an unharmonious character. I would rather drink a bottle of Asda's sparkling pinot noir chardonnay from Australia any day, at around £6, than any bottle of non-vintage Moet & Chandon at two-and-a-half times that price.

It is in this spirit that I have put this *Guide* together. I have tried to find all the inexpensive bargains among the eleven major supermarkets' 4000 wines, and I have earnestly striven to locate and praise those more expensive wines which are deserving of your patronage. Indeed, it is true to say that there are enough decent, interesting, individual wines between £4 and £8 to keep even the most critical of palates happy; certainly happy enough never again to have to fork out two, three or even four times those prices for so-called grand wines which are all-hype but at bottom no-hope.

Each supermarket in this *Guide* is separately listed with the wines arranged by country of origin, red and white (including rosés). Each wine's name is as printed on its label.

Each wine is rated on points out of 20. This system needs explaining, first from the viewpoint of the taster and then from yours, the drinker. As a taster I rate wines o to 20, always putting my mouth where your pocket is.

Rating a wine
An excellent supermarket wine can be so characterized because of its price, not only because it is good. Take as an example Domaine de Château Pigoudet, from Tesco. This

Provence wine rates 14 not just because it is gracefully balanced between fruitiness, dryness and acidity and so is well-made and highly drinkable, but because, at around the four quid mark, it is keenly priced. This wine would not rate 14 if it cost over a fiver, and certainly not if it cost, say, £7 or £8. The full scoring system, from the taster's point of view, works as follows:

20 Is outstanding and faultless in all departments: smell, taste and finish in the throat. Worth the price, even if you have to take out a second mortgage.

19 A superb wine. Almost perfect.

18 An excellent wine but lacking the depth and finesse for the top. Extremely good value.

17 An exciting, well-made wine at an affordable price.

16 Very good wine indeed. Good enough for *any* dinner party. Not expensive.

15 For the money, a good mouthful with real style.

14 The top end of everyday drinking wine. Well-made and to be seriously recommended at the price.

13 Good wine, true to its grape(s). Not great, but very drinkable.

12 Everyday drinking wine at a sensible price.

11 Drinkable, but not a wine to dwell on.

10 Average wine (at a low price), yet still a passable mouthful. Also, wines which are expensive and, though drinkable, do not justify their high price.

9 Cheap plonk. Fine for parties in dustbin-sized dispensers.

8 On the rough side. Chemicals showing through.

7 Good for pickled onions.

6 Hardly drinkable except on an icy night by a raging bonfire.

5 Wine with all its defects and mass manufacturing
   methods showing.
4 Not good at any price.
3 Barely drinkable.
2 Not to be recommended to anyone, even winos.
1 Beyond the pale. Awful. Even Lucretia Borgia
   wouldn't serve it.

The *Guide* concerns itself largely, though not exclusively, with wines which score 10 or more points (see page
xvi for how the scoring system works from your point of
view and how the *Guide* notates prices). Undoubtedly I will
have missed several wines which would be worthy of mention but which now lie on supermarket shelves to blush
unseen and unrated by me. This is especially true of wines
the supermarkets have brought out recently but which I
have been unable to taste in time. Also, you may find one
or two wines included which the supermarkets have only
just recently deleted. I would say, however, that this *Guide*
is as up-to-date as it is humanly possible to be.

Rating System

Scoring system

Anything scoring under 10 points is to be given a wide berth. Above the magic 10, the system works like this from your viewpoint:

10,11	Nothing nasty but equally nothing worth shouting from the rooftops. Drinkable.
12,13	Above average, interestingly made. A bargain taste.
14,15,16	This is the exceptional stuff, from the very good to the brilliant.
17,18	Really great wine worthy of individual acclaim. The sort of wine you can decant and serve to ignorant snobs who'll think it famous even when it is no such thing.
19,20	Bloody marvellous. Wine which cannot be faulted, providing an experience never to be forgotten.

Prices

I cannot guarantee the price of any wine in this *Guide* for all the usual boring reasons; inflation, economic conditions overseas, the narrow margins on some supermarket wines making it difficult to maintain consistent prices for very long and, of course, the existence of those freebooters at the Exchequer who are liable to up taxes which the supermarkets cannot help but pass on to the consumer. To get around this problem, a price banding code is assigned to each wine:

Price band

A	Under £2.50	D	£5–£7	G	£13–£20
B	£2.50–£3.50	E	£7–£10	H	Over £20
C	£3.50–£5	F	£10–£13		

Asda

The layout of Asda stores seems based on a very old Middle Eastern commercial concept: the bazaar. From toiletries to the fish counter, from the bread shelves to the booze, each section twinkles in its own way with its own individual style beckoning us to investigate. All that's missing, to continue the comparison with the inspired Arabic invention, is the traders themselves, ever welcoming, ever prepared to discuss a deal. Modern supermarketing is about *marketing*, not individual contact between seller and buyer. This means that the interior designer and the pack designer are crucial intermediaries between the store and the customer. With Asda, design principles have been carried further than with any other store. An Asda superstore is an exciting place to visit, for the jaded browser as well as the inveterate consumer. The individualization of certain sections of a store is a good idea.

As far as the wines are concerned, the individualization concentrates primarily on the labels rather than on any overt difference in layout or shelving. Personally, I think this is a pity. I would like to see sawdust on the floor, upturned barrels with candles, and an ancient Frenchman, yellow Gauloise parked permanently in his mouth, offering *dégustation gratuite* to the passing pram-pushers. Speaking not a word of comprehensible English, he would liven up proceedings even more and the kids would love him. He would, of course, be as baffled by many of the labels on the bottles as we are; but this only adds to the fun at Asda.

The banks of wines nictate like jewels; the natty labels enticing as sirens. Each and every bottle is irresistible –

never mind the contents. *En masse*, the effect of these heady designer containers is compelling. It seems impossible to suspect such considered typography and such seductive graphic imagery of hiding anything but the most sublime liquids. The question is, are they?

This is where the hidden talents of the store's wine-buying team enters the picture. For no matter how gloriously persuasive a label, if the wine is lousy, it will not grace our trolley a second time.

As the following entries demonstrate, Asda has a lot of interesting bottles on offer, the contents of which can stimulate debate as much as the labels themselves.

ARGENTINIAN WINE – *red*

Estancia Cabernet Sauvignon   13   £B
Dry to the point of thorniness yet finished in a fruity coat which agreeably packages the wine in the mouth. Very good value.

AUSTRALIAN WINE – *red*

Berri Estates, Cabernet Sauvignon/Shiraz 1986   14   £C
Terrific value to set a beef stew aflame with spice and richness.

Hardy's Premium Red   13   £B
Excellent value.

Longleat, Shiraz 1987   15   £E
A gorgeous peppered wine with depth, aromatic profundity
and a good deal of class. A gargantuan lump of leathery
rich fruit lies at the centre of the taste, surrounded by
charcoal. The wine has the most gloriously off-putting
label yet devised. The bottle would sit most comfortably in
a herbal doctor's surgery and may well cure all manner of
ills. It certainly banishes any blues the drinker may have.

Oxford Landing, Cabernet/Shiraz NV   13   £C
A little humdinger with its spicy acidity and richness of
fruit.

AUSTRALIAN WINE – *white*

Hunter Estate, Chardonnay 1988   12   £D
A clean finish, but still that pear-drop tang in the mouth
which denies the bottle the characteristic of unilateral
drinkability. Needs food and lots of fellow drinkers – one
glass is enough for me.

Old Triangle Riesling, Hill-Smith Estate
1988   12   £B

Oxford Landing, Chardonnay 1990   13   £C
This primly labelled beast is a most discreet and charming
wine with none of the tigerish tinned-pineapple grip of
some Aussie chardonnays.

Rosemount Wood-Matured Semillon
1987/88   12   £C

AUSTRIAN WINE – *white*

Lenz Moser, Beerenauslese 1984   12   £D
Nice with apple pie and custard, interestingly.

BULGARIAN WINE – *red*

Merlot   12   £A

CHILEAN WINE – *red*

Cabernet Sauvignon Viña Linderos 1987   12   £C
Fine value.

Cousino Macul, Cabernet Sauvignon 1987   13   £C

Viña Linderos, Cabernet Sauvignon 1987   13   £C
A touch like a St-Emilion in its integrated suppleness. Very
fruity (blackcurrant and raspberry) with a good finish.
Good value for a wine of such mature style. Dinner-party
stuff.

FRENCH WINE – *red*

**Beaujolais-Villages, Domaine de la Ronze
1989**   13   £C
A fruity beaujolais in *le style typique*. And good value at this

price these days (when beaujolais is outlandishly priced and rarely worth over a fiver).

Burgundy (Asda) 11 £C

Cabernet Sauvignon NV (Asda) 13 £B
If you require an easy drinking cabernet sauvignon for a casual dinner party, this is it. Not especially engaging aromatically, but soft and attractively fruity. Good value.

Caramany, Côtes du Roussillon Villages 1988 (magnum) 14 £D

Château Beauséjour, Côtes de Castillon 1986 12 £C

Château Bel Air, Bordeaux 1988 12 £D

Château de Cabriac, Corbières 1988 16 £D
A full, rich, dark wine with masses of fruit, elegant tannins and great style. By itself, it's reason enough to shop at Asda.

Château de Parenchère 12 £C

Château du Bois de la Garde, Côtes du Rhône 13 £C

Château Hanteillan 1988 13 £D
Classy assemblage here – good bouquet, firm body, excellent fruit.

Château Haut-Saric 1989 14 £B
Deserves to sell out at this price – good quaffing bordeaux with sufficient depth to be taken seriously. A mite mean aromatically, but at this price don't sniff, buy. The blend of grapes, and the proportions, match those of some of the great châteaux, so it's a proven recipe. The wine is exclusive to the store.

Château Le Gardera, Bordeaux 1987   12   £C
A hairy claret with an unforgiving demeanour – but give it
time and it'll be a talking-point: drink it three hours after
opening or, better yet, stick it away in a dark hole for a few
years.

Château Val-Joanis, Côtes du Lubéron 1988   12   £C

Claret (Asda)   12   £B

Côtes du Duras (Asda)   12   £A

Domaine de Barjac 1989   12   £B
This is an organic wine; stern, dry and excellent with roast
meat dishes.

**Domaine de Grangeneuve, Coteaux du
Tricastin**   12   £C

Fronton, Côtes Frontonnais (Asda)   14   £B
Excellent value for money for a full, rich wine.

Mâcon Supérieur (Asda)   11   £B

Moulin-à-Vent, Château des Jacques 1986   11   £E

St-Chinian (Asda)   13   £B
Bargain at under £3. Outstanding value for money for a
fruity, vat-aged plonk.

St-Emilion (Asda)   13   £C
This supple blend of merlot and cabernet franc is a typical
St-Emilion, making it an attractive luncheon wine.

St-Joseph 1988 (Asda)   12   £D

St-Joseph Cave de Tain 1987   12   £C
All syrah, this is a nicely made, blackcurrant rich wine.

Syrah, Vin de Pays des Collines Rhondaniennes 14 £C

An engaging mouthful of tobaccoey fruit and chewiness.

Vin de Pays des Côtes de Gascogne 12 £C

This is one of the wines the store is most proud of. And good quaffing stuff it is, with an attractive burnt bouquet. Very dry mouthful, with a slightly bitter background. I daresay it would be smashing with sausages blackened from the barbecue.

Volnay Domaine Henri Boillot 1986 13 £F

FRENCH WINE – *white*

Bergerac, Château la Jaubertie, 1989 13 £C

Made by the Ryman who flogged his stationery empire to go into wine-making – and how majestically he does it! (Though he has the help of a charming young Australian who knows exactly how to extract the right degree of fruitiness from the grapes.)

Burgundy (Asda) 11 £C

A reasonable stab at a simple burgundy but with an insubstantial bouquet; nevertheless the wine has fruit and a steely edge. Curious label of blue fish with which the wine does not go.

Cabernet de Saumur 13 £B

A delicate, delicious, good-value wine with strictly summery appeal.

Cabernet de Saumur, Rosé NV 13 £B

Good value, good fruit, good style.

Chablis 1988 (Asda)   12   £D

Chablis Grand Cru Bougros 1986   12   £G
This is a lot of money for a chablis which, though deliciously drinkable, narrowly fails to clamber on that band-
wagon called 'great'. The 1988 vintage will probably have
replaced the 1986 by the time this book goes to press.

Chablis Premier Cru 1987/88 Fourchamé   13   £E
Gorgeous wine, with the delicate, balanced finesse of fruit
and acidity that is typical of first-rate chablis. The bouquet
is lightly toasted, with a touch of lemon with sesame seeds
appearing in the taste. It is only a mite disappointing in the
finish which, perhaps inevitably, cannot quite live up to the
beginning. Lovely stuff, but expensive.

Coteaux du Layon, Domaine Touchais 1979   13   £D

Entre-Deux-Mers 1988/89   11   £A

Entre-Deux-Mers Château Fondarzac 1990   13   £C
A bright touch in this wine, elusive to nomenclature, gives
it a curious appeal. I dare say it would dazzle as an accompaniment to a healthy helping of fresh shellfish.

Muscat Cuvée Henry Peyrottes   15   £B
Marvellous individual dessert wine for almost any pud. A
touch of grilled molasses under the blowsy toffeed honey
gives it great presence in the mouth. Miraculous value for
money.

Muscat de Beaumes de Venise   14   £D
It strikes me that Beaumes de Venise has become so
consistent in its style and unchanging in what it delivers to
the drinker, particularly as an accompaniment to fresh soft
fruits, that it seems as if every bottle emanates from the

same maker. This one is no exception. Standard gorgeous drinking.

Muscat de Beaumes de Venise Les Trois Forêts 1987 (half) 15 £C
Lovely, individual dessert wine. Quite out of the ordinary, and its dash of zesty acidity makes it an exceptional Beaumes de Venise.

Pinot Blanc (Asda) 1989 12 £C

Sancerre, Château de Thauveney 1989 11 £D

Vin de Pays des Côtes de Gascogne 13 £C
The usual banana-and-peach aroma and taste, but nicely controlled in this example. Happy rustic hooch and a happy rustic price.

GERMAN WINE – *white*

Baden Dry (Asda) 12 £B
A German with a sense of humour? Not quite, but certainly an uncharacteristic German; dry and unfussily fruity and excellent with shellfish.

Bereich Bernkastel (Asda) 11 £B

Erdener Treppchen, Riesling Auslese 1985 14 £E
Astonishingly lemony pudding wine which is sensational with apple tart.

Herxheimer Honigsack Beerenauslese 12 £E

Mainzer Domherr (Asda)   14   £B
Superb little aperitif wine: fragrant, clean and cheap.

Niersteiner Rosenberg, Metternich, 1989   11   £C

Niersteiner Spiegelberg (Asda) 1989   11   £B

HUNGARIAN WINE – *red*

Merlot   13   £A
No mean wine for very mean people.

HUNGARIAN WINES – *white*

Gewürztraminer   5   £A
There are two partnerships it is wise to steer clear of: 1. an
angry orang-utan brandishing a Kalashnikov and 2. a
bottle of wine bearing the words Hungary and Gewürztraminer.

ITALIAN WINE – *red*

Bardolino (Asda)   12   £B

Bardolino NV   13   £B

Chianti Classico Riserva Villa Antorini 1986   14   £D
Only true chianti delivers sophistication and panache in a

paradoxically rustic style. This wine is typical: earthy, strong and fruity – but not cheap.

Ciro, Librandi 1988   14 £C
Maturely fruity and gorgeously teeth-gripping, like a fruit cake with fangs. Terrific with Italian food.

Montepulciano d'Abruzzo Bianchi 1988 14 £B
Yummy stuff.

ITALIAN WINE – *white*

Bianco di Custoza 1989   13 £C
Delicious, but perilously close to a fiver.

Chardonnay di Alto Adige (Asda)   14 £C
Well-made chardonnay with a clean finish. Nicely unfussy yet fruity, it can be drunk agreeably on its own or with food.

Lugana, Santa Christina 1989   14 £D
If the price of white burgundy is giving you a headache (like the wine itself can), then chuck your hard-earned dosh at this instead. Delicate, subtly flowery, and clean but thoroughly Northern Italian in manner: a fine Latin/ Alpine mix in both style and flavour. A splendid wine.

Verdicchio delle Marche   13 £B
Excellent soft fruit and clean acidity. Good value and great with fish.

LEBANESE WINE – *red*

Château Musar 1982   17 £D
A lovely balance of body, depth and quite volatile spiciness.
A distinguished wine with mature oaky character under the
fruit. I have to confess this is one of my favourite reds in
the book and I don't think I'm being romantic by virtue of
the fact that this has been, until the war in its country
stopped, the greatest red wine in the world made under
fire.

NEW ZEALAND WINE – *white*

Delegats, Sauvignon Blanc 1989   12 £D

**Delegats, Hawkes Bay, Sauvignon Blanc
1989**   11 £D
Grassy, bold and pricey – shellfish brings out the best in it.

PORTUGUESE WINE – *red*

Asda Douro 1988   13 £B
Ripe, well-muscled, impressively fruity – and easier to
swallow than Schwarzenegger. Good with rich foods and
cheeses.

Bairrada (Asda)   15 £B
Outstanding mix of fruit and wood-smoke makes this wine
marvellous with rich foods. The price is scandalously

cheap (Portugal seems to live a decade behind everyone else, price-wise).

Dão 1987   14   £B
A handsome bundle of attractive baked fruit. It cries out, or rather melodiously bawls, for food. Quite outstanding value.

PORTUGUESE WINE – *white*

Douro, Asda   13   £B
Excellent value for dinner parties, goes well with chicken in cream sauce.

SPANISH WINE – *red*

Don Darias   12   £B

Rioja Riserva, Santana 1986   13   £D
Delicious soft rioja – not a mouthful of oak shavings but a fistful of well-finessed fruit.

Torres Coroñas 1985   13   £C
Señor Torres really is a magician – he produces marvellous mouthfuls of wine which can compete with bottles costing much more. Silky and rich and excellent with roast foods, this example of his sorcery.

Viña Albali Valdepeñas Gran Reserva 1984   14   £B
Midget price for a mighty mature wine. One of the wine bargains of the century.

USA WINE – *red*

Colombia, Pinot Noir 1987   15 £D
Under seven quid, this has to be one of the most impressive pinot noirs on sale. Its major competition is not from
Burgundy but from Oregon and California, of the same
1987 vintage. Woody, gamy, scrumptious fruit, held in
check by the characteristic vegetal pinot noir framing, it is
a bargain wine for serious pinot freaks. This wine makes
me wish my nearest Asda was round the corner and not
half-an-hour's drive away.

USA WINE – *white*

Essensia Orange Muscat Quady 1988   13 £D
Acquired taste – the name accurately describes its effect
on the taste-buds.

SPARKLING WINE/CHAMPAGNE

Australian Pinot Noir Chardonnay NV   14 £D
A big mouthful of mature fruit. More appealing than many
a raw champagne at twice the price.

Cava (Asda)   12 £C

Cava Brut (Asda)   12 £C
A product marred only by the finish in the throat which

disappoints. But many folk will buy it for the splendidly pretentious bottle.

Champagne Brut (Asda)	12 £F

Champagne Rosé Brut (Asda)	14 £F

Crémant de Bourgogne (Asda)   13 £D
Why bother with the pretentions of Rheims when Burgundy makes this fine little sparkler?

Hungarian Chardonnay   10 £C
Like a dry Asti – peachy and fruity but not a lot more to write home about.

Moscatel de Valencia (Asda)   16 £B
Same score as Tesco, Waitrose, etc. who have this wine from Vincente Gandia. Marvellous stuff – liquid nougat, toffee and honey. Pleasant wine of huge panache at bargain price.

Budgen

Budgen is looking brighter-cheeked these days, as though it's spent time at a health farm. A designer has been at work on many of the in-store labels, the shelf layouts are more appealing, and the selection of wines is broader, with several interesting wines from uncommon areas.

This is mainly the work of a wine buyer who has since left to go to Safeway. However, her ideas and buying skills are in evidence on the shelves with several worthy items and, frankly, there isn't a lot more I can usefully say about the store except to thank it for not abandoning its car-less customers as some of the big boys seem to have done. Where I live, the retired folk are grateful they can walk to the local Budgen whereas the superstores require a bus-ride, or personal transport, to reach.

It is worth speculating upon the thought that with the huge slump in car sales and the general urban disfavour into which the motor car has fallen, stores like Budgen with their inner city positionings might well reap a consumer bonus early in the next century. This will be especially true if more and more big city dwellers chuck their cars for an improved public transport system and the car parks of the suburban superstores get turned into open markets and tennis courts. This may be cloud-cuckoo-land theorizing at the moment, but so was Einstein's once and look where that got him.

AUSTRALIAN WINE – *red*

Jacob's Creek Dry Red	11	£B

FRENCH WINE – *red*

Château Haut Tuquet 1985	13	£C
Delas Crozes Hermitage	10	£C
Faugères, Jean Jean	11	£A
Vin de Pays des Coteaux de l'Ardèche 1990	11	£B

You need a beak as long as the woodcock on the label to catch the bouquet, but thereafter the wine's drinkable enough. Good value for large numbers of drunks.

FRENCH WINE – *white*

Chablis Domaine St-Marc 1988	10	£D
Chardonnay, Domaine les Terres Blanches 1989	13	£C

Eric and Chris – nice one.

Château Fondarzac	12	£B
Château La Nère 1988 (half)	12	£B

Messieurs Dulac et Seraphon make a pleasant half of Loupiac, usefully sized for four people and a couple of punnets of strawberries. Not as luscious or as 'lissom'

(which is how the French describe Loupiac dessert wines)
as it might be, but engaging for all that.

Château le Gardera	11	£C

Corbières, Blanc de Blancs 1990   13   £B
Outright bargain. Not as determinedly keen-edged as it
might be, but attractively fruity in a quiet way all the same.

Domaine de Grandchamp 1989   13   £D
Made by the Englishman who flogged off Ryman the
stationers and found paradise in Bergerac. This wine is not
cheap for the style, but it is nicely put together and has a
better, and more harmonious, level of fruitiness than many
dry whites from the area. Stylish in a quaint way.

Gewürztraminer 1986	13	£C

Muscadet sur Lie, Beauregard 1989	11	£B

Pinot Blanc Gisselbrecht 1986	14	£C

Pinot d'Alsace, Willy Gisselbrecht 1988   14   £C
An excellent dry, fruity wine with a heart of steel. A fine
aperitif, supreme with grilled fish.

Sancerre, Les Grandes Dames 1989   11   £D
As like a truc sancerre as a pair of my socks. Unlike my
socks, however, the wine is not woolly and disagreeably
smelly, but merely pleasantly plonkish without the chic one
is entitled to expect in a wine costing this money calling
itself sancerre.

Touraine Sauvignon, Château Vieux	12	£B

Tuilerie du Bosc, Côtes de St-Mont 1990   13   £B
Softened in oak, yet with the firm freshness of youth – a
pleasant wine all round.

HUNGARIAN WINE – *red*

Merlot   11   £B

ITALIAN WINE – *red*

Castelli, Romani   10   £B

Chianti del Colle 1990   12   £C

ITALIAN WINE – *white*

Lugana, Villa Flora 1989   14   £C
The best white wine for the dosh in the whole store? (Only
Gisselbrecht with his pinot blanc has an argument ready-
bottled.) Certainly the Zenato family who make this wine
rarely seem to put a foot wrong as they stamp out one
elegant wine after another on Lake Garda's shores. This
one is beautifully clean and fresh, yet the fruit is sheer
citric velvet – a lovely thing to behold in the glass. And,
more importantly, to drink.

SPANISH WINE – *red*

Cune Reserva Rioja 1985   13   £D
Good value for a rioja of this age and non-hysterical
richness.

El Morano Valencia	11	£B

Rioja Viña Real 1987	11	£C

Torres Coroñas	12	£C

Torres, it seems, couldn't make a bad wine even if they tried.

Viña Albali 1984	14	£B

A bargain at the price – a mature, curranty rich wine for highly flavoured foods, or keep it as a surprise to go with cheese, even stilton.

SPANISH WINE – *white*

La Mancha 1990	12	£B

Made from the world's most prodigious grape variety – yet one which only the Spanish seem to have heard of. In this example, the grape turns in a surprisingly fresh performance.

USA WINE – *white*

Colombia Crest 1986	13	£D

Curious wine, with peaches and prickly pears humming away softly in the background. Mature, too, at five years old. Gives the jaded tongue something to think about after a hard day's work.

SPARKLING WINE/CHAMPAGNE

Chapain et Landais Grand Saumur	12	£D
Chapain et Landais Sparkling Rosé	12	£C

Co-op

The original idea behind the Co-op was terrific. Every customer had a share in the business, with every penny he or she spent contributing towards a regular dividend payout. (This quaint and wondrous custom still lives on in a few Co-op branches, I believe.) The more you spent, the more you received. This was true whether you bought a Granny Smith at the Co-op greengrocer or buried one through the Co-op undertakers, the Co-op being the nation's most prolific interer of bodies, with 41 per cent of the business.

Nowadays, however, a different kind of partnership exists between the big stores and their customers. This is, first, to do with perceived value for money (that is, the store is selling certain staple items for as little as it possibly can and provides good value on other things). Second, but increasingly more importantly over the past decade, the stuff on the shelves is not only of a high quality but is as wholesome as possible. Nasty additives and obnoxious colourings, unnecessary sweeteners or unsavoury flavourings, are out; packaging which harms the environment, either during its manufacture or as a result of its disposal, is to be condemned; products tested on animals are frowned upon; and even imports from politically unacceptable countries like South Africa get short shrift. In other words, major stores enter into an emotional, not merely a commercial, partnership with their customers. The stores understand the way we feel. They are not merely faceless purveyors of the things that they sell; they are, they tell us, caring, sympathetic individuals like the rest of us, living off the same resources on the same planet. This carries the basis for a more enduring partnership than one based on a dividend cheque.

The Co-op, surprising though it may seem to those who shop elsewhere, recognizes this and, in some respects, cottoned on to some of the trends in food safety earlier than most. The store's Food Research Laboratory, for instance, has had claims made for it which put it on a par with even Marks & Spencer's.

But to the inquisitive wine buyer this commitment counts for little if the wines in this *Guide* are nowhere to be seen when he wanders into his local Co-op. And here we have the nub of the Co-op's marketing problem: it is light years behind the Tescos and the Sainsburys and the Safeways who have single-minded objectives carried out by clearly briefed staff.

The dear old Co-op is clearly out of date in this respect. It cannot enforce a strict marketing style and selling pattern on all its stores because it cannot enforce centralized buying. An individual Co-op may have none of the wines in this list or it may have all of them. Annoyingly, it may have just one or two. Co-ops are free to buy from whatever source they care to. The vast buying power of the Co-op as a whole, therefore, which, with its 4000 outlets around the country, should command enormous clout, is not utilized as effectively as it could be. If every Co-op shop with wine shelves boasted the same range of wines, the savings to the customer would be phenomenal.

Not that Co-op wines are pricey. Far from it. Take a look at the cheap whites and reds from Italy, for example; they are all decent wines and all decently priced. You'll find other worthy bottles here, too. The Co-op's champagne is no mean fizzer and there are some handsome Aussie reds.

When the day comes that all that skill and enthusiasm in the wine buying department is channelled into a coherent, workable marketing strategy, the Co-op could become a force to rank alongside the Sainsburys and the Tescos.

AUSTRALIAN WINE – *red*

Cabernet Sauvignon 1987 13 £C
Terrific with roast turkey and stuffing of dried fruits.

Shiraz 14 £C
Minty, tarry, fruity – good New World style. Very good value.

AUSTRALIAN WINE – *white*

Columbard and Chardonnay 1987 11 £C

Semillon 12 £C

Semillon 1990 12 £C
Incisive attack from the melony fruit. Keen defence from the citric acidity.

BULGARIAN WINE – *red*

Cabernet Sauvignon 11 £B

BULGARIAN WINE – *white*

Riesling and Misket   12   £B

CHILEAN WINE – *red*

Cabernet Sauvignon   12   £B

ENGLISH WINE – *white*

English Table Wine   11   £C
Not so much rounded as humpbacked and spineless – not
altogether ugly, though. The blend of German grapes
works well and a glass is a pleasant end to a day's work and
an evening's entertainment.

FRENCH WINE – *red*

Anjou Rouge (Pierre Chaumont)   12   £B
This wine is made from an undervalued grape called
cabernet franc which is not to be confused with the famous
cabernet sauvignon. This franc devaluation is to the wine-
drinker's advantage, for it makes very interesting and
good-value wine in the Anjou area of France, in particular
Bourgeuil and Chinon. This Anjou is not in their class but
nevertheless it has some of the rustic charm of its most

illustrious cousins; this is especially in evidence in the bouquet, which has the distinct hint of lead pencils. The taste, however, is not as unappetizing as it sounds, being fruity, dry and reasonably rounded. Anjou rouge can be drunk to advantage chilled, like beaujolais.

Bergerac Rouge (Pierre Chaumont) 13 £B

Bergerac first found fame with the eponymous Cyrano, but his length of nose is unnecessary with so forward a bouquet as this wine exhibits. A country plonk, yes, but with a mite more character and backbone than many, and this is reflected in the rating. It also has an agreeably fruity finish; unlike some rural simpletons it does not imagine its job is over once you have swilled it around the mouth. Good with roasts and hearty dinners, it has, nevertheless, enough going for it to be drunk on its own.

Charles Vienot Côtes de Beaune Villages 12 £D

Château Cissac 1982 12 £E

Château Cissac 1984 11 £E

Château du Piras (Pierre Chaumont) 14 £C

A proper structure to this wine gives it a typical petit-bordeaux style, with its fruitiness held firmly in check by an attractive, dry edge. It also has an immediate matey quality, unlike so many bordeaux with their stiff-mannered approach demanding years of ageing and hours of breathing before they agree to embrace you as a drinking companion.

Claret (Pierre Chaumont) 12 £B

Corbières (Pierre Chaumont) 11 £B

Coteaux du Tricastin (Pierre Chaumont)   12   £B
This wine comes from a pleasant French town called
Valréas, where Rhône bargains are often to be unearthed.
This is a simple, gulpable, fruity yet dry wine with no mean
characteristics whatsoever. It cannot set the universe
ablaze, but it would agreeably set off sausages and mash
with a healthy dollop of mustard.

Côtes de Provence Rouge (Pierre Chaumont)	12	£B
Côtes du Rhône (Pierre Chaumont)	11	£B
Côtes du Roussillon (Pierre Chaumont)	11	£A
Côtes de Ventoux (Pierre Chaumont)	11	£B
Fitou (Pierre Chaumont)	12	£B

Mâcon Rouge (Pierre Chaumont)   12   £C
Not a bad stab at burgundy plonk. A friendly, authentic-
tasting mâcon which is a more approachable Burgundian
than more expensive examples from the same designated
area. It has a pleasant, though slightly grassy, bouquet, an
ample amount of dryish fruit, and a little tickle on the
throat as it goes down reminiscent of its neighbour's pride
and joy, beaujolais. Will go happily with uncomplicated
meat dishes or ghastly things like quiches.

Médoc (Pierre Chaumont)	12	£C
Vin de Pays de l'Aude	11	£A
Vin de Table Red	11	£A

FRENCH WINE – *white*

Alsace Gewürztraminer (Pierre Chaumont)   11   £C

Alsace Pinot Blanc (Pierre Chaumont)   14   £B
This is an extremely well-put-together example of pinot
blanc, a grape variety which often results in wine of such
great acidity that it screams out for food. Not so with this
French example: a pleasant, flowery bouquet leading to a nice
balance of dryness and acidic fruitiness. Not surprisingly,
this is one of the wines the wine buyer is most proud of.

Alsace Riesling (Pierre Chaumont)   10   £B

Anjou Blanc (Pierre Chaumont)   13   £B

Bergerac Blanc (Pierre Chaumont)   11   £B

Blanc de Blancs   11   £B

**Bordeaux Blanc Medium Dry (Pierre
Chaumont)**   12   £B

Bourgogne Blanc (Pierre Chaumont)   10   £D

Côtes de Provence Rosé (Pierre Chaumont)   10   £B

Gallière Sauternes 1988   11   £E

**Premières Côtes de Bordeaux (Pierre
Chaumont)**   11   £B

Rosé d'Anjou (Pierre Chaumont)   12   £A
A goodish, firm little rosé.

Sauvignon Blanc (Pierre Chaumont)   11   £B

Vin de Pays d'Oc Sauvignon Blanc   13   £B

Vin de Pays de la Vallée du Paradis – Grenache	13	£B
Vin de Pays des Côtes de Gascogne	12	£B
Vin de Pays des Côtes Catalanes	13	£A

A very good wine for this sort of money. Fruity and not without some style.

| Vin de Pays des Côtes des Pyrénées Orientales | 13 | £B |

GERMAN WINE – *white*

Bereich Niestein (Lohengrin)	12	£A
Bernkasteler Kurfustlay (Lohengrin)	12	£A
Deidesheimer Hofstuck Kabinett 1988	13	£B
Hock Deutscher Tafelwein	11	£A
Klusserather St-Michael (Lohengrin)	13	£A
Liebfraumilch (Lohengrin)	10	£A
Model Deutscher Tafelwein	11	£A
Moseltaler (Lohengrin)	11	£B
Niersteiner Gutes Domtal (Lohengrin)	13	£A
Oppenheimer Krotenbrunnen (Lohengrin)	11	£A
Piesporter Michelsberg (Lohengrin)	12	£B
Rudesheimer Rosengarten (Lohengrin)	12	£A

Urziger Schwarzlay Spätlese 12 £C

The wine's flowery fruitiness and acidity make it what most people will characterize as sweet. It is well-made and has some charm, but it has insufficient flesh to go with main-course food, and its fruitiness is too puny to tackle desserts.

Zeller Schwarze Katz (Lohengrin) 10 £B

ITALIAN WINE – *red*

Barolo Roche 1984 11 £D

Chianti 1990 10 £B

Otto Santi Chianti Classico 1987 13 £D

Big woody aroma reminiscent of a rioja, but with just enough of its grape variety's (sangiovese) tannin to give it that subtle bitterness bequeathed to the Tuscan by virtue of climate, sun and soil.

Valpolicella (Carissa) 12 £A

ITALIAN WINE – *white*

Frascati (Carissa) 10 £B

Orvieto Secco (Carissa) 12 £C

Typical orvieto with its acidic, citric finish. This hints at a certain zestiness in the wine which is best with fish.

| Soave (Carissa) | 10 | £A |
| Verdicchio Classico (Carissa) | 12 | £C |

PORTUGUESE WINE – *red*

Bairrada 1987   14 £B
Decant it some hours beforehand and let your guests think
it's some old thing the family's been hanging on to. When
they tuck into their roast beef with onion sauce and drink
the wine they'll just coo . . .

Dão 1988   13 £B
Big and rich yet surprisingly youthful. Good with ham
dishes.

PORTUGUESE WINE – *white*

Bairrada 1989   12 £B
Clean and nutty and fresh – but even Inspector Morse
couldn't find who kidnapped the fruit.

| Portuguese Rosé | 10 | £B |
| Portuguese Vinho Verde | 11 | £B |

SPANISH WINE – *red*

| Full-Bodied Red (St-Marcus) | 13 | £B |

Gran Condol Rioja Reserva 1984   13 £D
The creamy, vanilla quality of this wine can be quite
objectionable in some circumstances, like overlipsticked
lips, but in this case the effect is lovely. One of the few red
wines I can imagine wrestling with chicken tikka and living
to tell the tale.

Dry White (St-Marcus)   10 £A

Medium White (St-Marcus)   10 £B

SPARKLING WINE/CHAMPAGNE

Cava   11 £C

De Clairveaux Brut Champagne   13 £F
Yeasty and fruity.

De Clairveaux Rosé Champagne   12 £G
If you must drink such things, this is as reasonable a wine
as any other at the price, but that price is high.

Sekt (Lohengrin)   11 £B

Gateway/Somerfield

This store will surprise you. Can you credit the fact that it stocks a drinkable Chinese chardonnay? A marvellous 15-point Australian red? Several interesting *petit château* wines from Bordeaux? And some interesting reds from the Rhone Valley?

All this is apart from an interesting range of cheap white wines, most of them extremely good value for money.

Gateway's move into bigger things with its Somerfield shops is good news, too. Especially for customers who like the layout of a wine department to be friendly yet professional-looking. And the most heartening sign here is the signing up of wine buyer Angela Mount from Safeway. Her enthusiasm and dedication are beginning to bear fruit. The wines mentioned above are a testimony to her buying skills.

The result is that Gateway *is* a place to buy wine now, not just the shop to pop into for the ketchup and the floor cleaner. The full range, however, is more likely to be found in a large Somerfield store than a smaller Gateway.

AUSTRALIAN WINE – *red*

Somerfield Australian Grenache Shiraz (Somerfield)   14   £B
Outstanding value – dry yet fruity, faintly spicy.

Berri Estates Cabernet Sauvignon/Shiraz 1987   14   £C
Marvellous forward stuff. A touch ripe on the fruit but with nosh, gosh!

CHINESE WINE – *white*

Tsingtao Chinese Chardonnay   12   £C
(See Sainsbury's.) Basically this is a typical Australian
chardonnay. At £4.99 it's expensive. Perhaps too expensive.
But it's worth 12 points and bags of curiosity value.

FRENCH WINE – *red*

Bourgogne Pinot Noir 1988   12   £C

Château de Caraguilhes 1989   13   £B
Big, brawny, organic stuff. Keep for a year and it'll be even
better.

Château de Quilhanet 1989   13   £A

Château la Menardie 1989   13   £C

Château La Terrasse, Côtes de Castillon   13   £C
A mature bordeaux, typically tannic, but showing no
graceless hardness. Very good value.

Château St-Justin, Côtes du Rhône 1989   13   £C
Another Lancon production of a possible declassified
Châteauneuf-du-Pape contender. Grenache, cinsault, mourvèdre and syrah make a handsome if not perfectly integrated
bunch – the result is a fruity wine of bite and depth.

Château St-Robert, Graves 1987   13   £C
Nice style, nice price. Dry and fruity, with a distant hint of
the cedarwood aroma of fine Graves.

Châteauneuf du Pape La Jacquinotte   13   £C
This is tough, chewy, but very attractive – due, I think, to the

mourvèdre grape variety's inclusion in the blend. It is a full wine, not immediately fruity, but very approachable if you don't mind the absence of the softness this wine normally demonstrates. Good with roast foods.

Claret (Somerfield)	13	£B
Côtes de Gascogne	12	£A
Côtes du Roussillon Villages 1989	12	£B

Nice touch of stalky richness.

Domaine des Garbes 1980	13	£C

Excellent value for a pudding wine of this style.

Domaine Fontarney 1979	13	£E

I've had bottles of this particular wine maturing in my coal-hole since 1983. It was awful then – it needed to unbung its closed bouquet and release its fruit. Now it's ready and Gateway have it at a reasonable price (it is after all the second wine of Château Brane-Cantenac, third-growth St-Estèphe, and it is made by one of Bordeaux's most impressive wine makers, André Lurton). The fruit is still restrained, austere almost, but it's an elegant though stiffly mannered wine, with a distinguished claret feel. Very good with dinner-party roasts.

Médoc	11	£B
Minervois, Jean Jean	12	£A

FRENCH WINE – *white*

Beaujolais 1990 (Somerfield)	11	£C

Bordeaux Sauvignon 1990 (Somerfield) 12 £B

Chais Baumière Chardonnay 1990 12 £C
What do Australians get up to in the South of France? Drink
this and find out – they make themselves at home.

Château du Chayne 1990 13 £C
Marvellous with shellfish. Lovely melony/lemony fruit.

Château du Queyret 1990 13 £B

Château Tour de Montredon 1990 11 £B

**Domaine de Marignan VDP, Côtes de Thau
1990** 12 £B

Domaine du Petit Bosc 1990 13 £C
Goodness, doesn't the Gateway wine buyer know her white
wines!

Graves 1990 (Somerfield) 13 £B

Hautes Côtes de Beaune 1989 12 £D
Pleasant touch of gaminess on the soft fruitiness. White
burgundy at a reasonable price.

Montagny Premier Cru 1989 12 £D

**Vin de Pays des Coteaux de L'Ardèche
Blanc** 13 £B
Terrific value. Very clean, not a lot of fruit. Good with
shellfish.

GERMAN WINE – *white*

St-Johanner Abtei 1988 12 £B

**St-Ursula Weinkellerei Bingen Morio
Muskat** 11 £A

**St-Ursula Weinkellerei Bingen Pinot Blanc
Trocken Gallerei Range** 11 £B

**St-Ursula Weinkellerei Bingen Rheingau
Riesling** 11 £B

HUNGARIAN WINE – *red*

Bull's Blood 1984 14 £B
A corker of a wine for £2.75 and six years of age. In this
period the fruit has matured (almost, some would say,
over-ripened) and blended well with the wood flavours from
the oak barrels. The result is a wine of no great complexity
but effortlessly rounded richness. A bargain at the price,
terrific with roasts, spicy or rich foods.

ITALIAN WINE – *red*

Barolo, Castiglione Faletto 1986 12 £D
A chewy, chocolate biscuit-rich wine. Excellent with
pungent foods.

Chianti, Conti Serristori 1989 13 £B
Go for its dry earthy fruitiness, curranty richness and almost
ripe dryness. With a vast bowl of garlicky pasta and lots of
friends around the table, the wine is superb.

ITALIAN WINE – *white*

Caldeo 1990   13   £B
Lemons and raspberries – a subtle fruit salad set off by a
dash of Venetian acidity. Delicious value for money.

**Chardonnay del Piemonte 1990, Viticoltori
dell Acquese**   13   £B
A very fresh chardonnay, with the fruit cutting a dash rather
than the acidity. Great with fish and chicken.

**Frascati, Principe Pallavicini 1990
(Somerfield)**   12   £C
Fresh and gently nutty – if that makes the wine sound like an
eccentric nymphomaniac, I apologize to it.

Montereale 1990   13   £B
You can't grumble at the price, bitch at this much pleasant
fruitiness, or complain about the streak of fresh acidity. I
know this sounds like every other white wine at around this
price at Gateway, but the store's wine buyer has a magic
touch with such bottles, and the only problem they present is
how to describe each one with originality.

Pinot Grigio del Veneto 1990   13   £B
Delicious.

Prunalbo 1988   12   £C
Elegance, a touch of coffee/chocolate – unusual but very
agreeable. Made to stand on candlelit dinner tables.

Terre di Ginestra 1990   13   £C
For a fuller description of this wine, see Tesco.

SPANISH WINE – *red*

Don Hugo 13 £B
Very fruity and instantly likeable.

Viña Albali Riserva 1984 14 £B
Ridiculous that a seven-year-old wine can cost just over £3.
It's creamy, vanilla-ey, blackcurranty, and rather forceful.
Drink with equally characterful dishes.

SPANISH WINE – *white*

Penedès Blanco 1990 13 £B
Very attractive balance of fruit and acid.

Rioja 1988 (Somerfield) 11 £C

Somontano Montesierra 1990 13 £B
Outstanding little chardonnay-type wine. Excellent value –
delicious fruitiness allied to tongue-tingling cleanness.

Valencia Dry White 13 £B
Outstanding value for money. Dry, fruity, simple and
gluggable.

USA WINE – *white*

Sebastiani Chardonnay 1990 12 £C

**Washington State Semillon Chardonnay
1989** 13 £C
Charmingly subtle partnership of two rich grape varieties.

SPARKLING WINE/CHAMPAGNE

Chardonnay Santi Vino Spumante Brut   13   £C
Excellent aperitif sparkler.

Chardonnay Spumante   12   £D

Crémant de Bourgogne   12   £D
Excellent structure. Good balance. Very good value.

Moscato Fizz   13   £A
Not strictly wine at 4.75 per cent alcohol. Under two quid a
bottle, though, so who's going to bitch? Terrific stuff for
teenage parties with lots of ice-cream.

Raimat Chardonnay Brut   14   £D
Can't afford mature vintage champagne? Fear not. Stick
your nose in a glass of this and then swig and forget Rheims
ever existed.

Vouvray, Tête de Cuvée   14   £D
Knock-out champagne sub. Makes an admirable pre-
dinner come-on.

Wiltinger Sharzberg Riesling 1987   13   £C
Great for summer garden parties, with its bubbly
peachiness.

Littlewoods

Most people will be surprised to see that this store is even represented in this *Guide*. I have nothing to add which will mollify or enhance this sense of surprise so you can either continue to walk past your local Littlewoods with your nose in the air, or you can nip in there with this hot little book in your fist. A visit will at least change your mind about a name you thought only appeared on pools coupons and in clothes catalogues.

AUSTRALIAN WINE – *red*

Jacob's Creek Red	13	£B
Jacob's Creek Dry Red	13	£C

Full-bodied, but not too over-developed – complementary to carnivores' favourites like steak and onions.

AUSTRALIAN WINE – *white*

Jacob's Creek Medium Dry White	11	£B

BULGARIAN WINE – *red*

Bulgarian Cabernet Sauvignon	12	£B

FRENCH WINE – *red*

Château d' Aigueville 1989   13 £C
Country wine at a bargain price: fruity, dry, rounded, with
agreeably complete structure. The sort of bottle which is
typical of the sunny Rhône in its suggestion of burliness
under the fruitiness.

Merlot de Caumont   10 £B

Vin de Table Red (Littlewoods)   12 £A

FRENCH WINE – *white*

Château d'Aigueville 1989   13 £C
This is a dry wine of some character and agreeable fruitiness. Good value.

**Domaine de San de Guilhem, Vin de Pays des Côtes
de Gascogne**   14 £B
Smashing bargain at under three quid: full and fruity in the
Gascony manner (rather like its most famous son
D'Artagnan) yet not so aggressively that a compensating
streak of dryness isn't pleasantly evident.

Rosé d'Anjou (Littlewoods)   13 £A

Vin de Table Dry (Littlewoods)   10 £A

Vin de Table Medium (Littlewoods)   10 £A

GERMAN WINE – *white*

Hock	11	£A

Morio Muskat	14	£A

A simple aperitif of remarkable acid/fruit balance. Outstanding value for money.

Moselle	11	£A

St-Johanner Abtei Auslese	12	£C

A glass is fine before a meal or, with a mild tart or hard fruit, after one.

HUNGARIAN WINE – *red*

Cabernet Sauvignon	12	£A

ITALIAN WINE – *red*

Chianti 1988	12	£B

A good-value rustic representative. Chews a straw and swears a bit but it is an agreeable chianti for all that.

Valpolicella	7	£B

So thin, and so quickly does the fruit flash across the palate, that they must have made it out of greyhounds.

ITALIAN WINE – *white*

Frascati	12 £B
A good aperitif wine.	

Soave	12 £B

PORTUGUESE WINE – *red*

Bairrada   14   £B
Very good value – a curranty, rich wine lending great
distinction to any dish. Excellent with nuts.

Dão   14   £B
This has all the typical characteristics of a well-made Dão.
Chocolatey, fruity yet dry, and excellent value for money.

SPANISH WINE – *red*

Rioja, Tondeluna 1986   14   £C
At a mite over £3.50, this is a bargain. A creamy, aromatic,
full-throated rioja it may be, but the vanilla flavouring from
the wood ageing is not criminal (as with many riojas) and
the fruitiness is herbal and mature. Excellent with rich
foods and spicy pastas.

SPARKLING WINE/CHAMPAGNE

Asti Martini   10   £D
Terribly sweet young thing.

Estrella   10   £B

Flutelle Blanc de Blancs Brut   10   £C

Kupferberg Gold   10   £D

Monsigny Champagne (Littlewoods)   11   £F
Solid rather than exciting.

Marks and Spencer

I was told by a co-operative wine-maker in France that there was only one posse of food and wine technologists more ornery than Sainsbury's and Tesco's and that was the bunch from Marks and Sparks. And Sparks seems the right name here for I suspect they fly in all directions if things do not meet the company's quality inspectors' standards. Of all the stores, this is the one in which the ethos of the own-label reaches its most powerful expression. No matter that you see a wine here with the same name as one at another supermarket; somehow the impression is given that the M & S version is uniquely its own. And this is true right down to the muesli and the smoked salmon. Somewhere, you think to yourself, knowing the thought to be utterly ridiculous, there is an old farm hand wearing a St. Michael badge on his overalls scything M & S oats to make M & S muesli and on some North Sea smack, called the *St Michael*, a grizzled M & S fisherman catches M & S salmon.

But how can this be true of wine? M & S can't make its own wine, can it? Of course we know it doesn't, but we buy the idea that it *as good as* makes its own wine through its attitude to what it buys. And, if my co-op wine-maker is to be believed, this is borne out in fact.

It is this image of high standards, enforced by having only one brand on sale, which has given the store a tremendous advantage. M & S could, in fact, get away with pricing many of its wines higher than they are without anyone complaining. The store's clientele don't shop exclusively on price; they go for value for money. An excellent wine, like the Bourgogne Epineuil, for example, could sell for pounds more in spite of being over a fiver to begin with.

It has, then, been encouraging to see the store concentrate on the cheaper end of the market over the past year or so. The M & S country wine range is good value for money and they have some red and white wines from the south of France that are not bettered, penny for penny, anywhere else. They even have a marvellous keenly priced champagne substitute from Alsace.

If I was running the marketing department at M & S (and doubtless a shudder is running through the company at the mere thought) I would push these wines for all I was worth with commercials during 'Coronation Street' if supplies permitted. These wines are so good, and so reasonably priced, that competitors might feel a chill.

You can find all of these wines in the listings which follow. And when you visit the store and pick up that elegantly labelled bottle of Côtes de Saint Mont for a laughable £2.99 and congratulate yourself on your good fortune, don't be silly and blow your money on an M & S dressed lobster at all of a tenner. The wine will go beautifully with the crustacean even though it's a third of the price.

FRENCH WINE – *red*

Abbaye des Tholomies, Minervois 1986   13   £B
Currants and ripe berries combine, in precise echoes of the syrah and grenache grape varieties the wine is made from. A nice, plump, mature little wine to enjoy with a

nice, plump, mature little chicken (roasted). Good value
for a five-year-old.

Bouches du Rhône   10   £A

Bourgogne Epineuil 1988   12   £D
This is an interesting wine. The appellation is a neglected
one, only recently enjoying a revival (thirty years ago only
one grower made the stuff). Made by La Chablisienne
co-op which turns out such terrific chablis for M & S, this
is a burgundy which will, I reckon, get better and better.

Bourgogne Pinot Noir 1989   11   £C

Cabernet Sauvignon   11   £B

Château de Beaulieu 1988   12   £B

Château Fonfroide 1990   13   £C
Clean and with enough fruit to be on the rich side, yet very
dry, this wine is vinified by freelance travelling wine-maker
Hugh Ryman (son of Nick, who flogged his stationery
empire to buy a French vineyard). The grapes are semillon
and sauvignon, picked early for their acidity and then
fermented in the modern style at low temperature for
maximum freshness.

Châteauneuf-du-Pape les Couvesets 1987   12   £E

Claret AC   14   £C
Excellent value. Decant it and it will surprise the neigh-
bours when you have them in for a simple supper.

Comte Tolosan 1990   14   £B
A love affair between two grape varieties (jurançon and
gamay) and, perhaps, the same relationship between
Marie-Paule Colombie and Gilles Berty of the co-op near

the banks of the river Tarn which makes this marvellous
bargain red. Certainly it seems that love has gone into this
wine. Truly, penny for penny, it is better drinking than any
beaujolais you care to lay your hands on. I drank a bottle
watching the men's final at Wimbledon on TV and I had a
smashing time.

Côtes de Gascogne	11	£B

Côtes de St-Mont 1988   14   £B
With cabernet franc and cabernet sauvignon grapes in the
recipe along with the less fashionable tannat and the
parochial fer servadou grape varieties, this is an interestingly handsome specimen, fruitily oaky and soft. It has
sufficient guts to age even more gracefully if kept for two
more years, and anyone taking this gamble would be well
rewarded. However, it is an utterly drinkable bottle right
now.

Côtes du Rhône   14   £C
Firm, fruity and a lovely southern mouthful.

**Domaine de L'Escattes, Vin de Pays de la
Vaunage 1989**   13   £B
Dryish and restrained; a light wine, but good value.

Domaine des Mélanies, Corbières 1989	13	£B

Fitou 1988	10	£B

Fleurie 1989   11   £E
I adore beaujolais, and a cru like Fleurie especially. But at
this price, I'd think twice. This wine, delicious though it is,
is rather more expensive than one might expect it to be.

French Country   10   £A

Full Red Côtes du Roussillon   12   £B

Gamay   12   £B

**Jean-Louis Chancel, Vin de Pays de Vaucluse
1989**   14   £B
This lovely blend of fruit and dryness makes a very impressive marriage.

La Grange Neuve de Figeac 1985   14   £E
This is a secondary product of an old Bordeaux vineyard which has always come up with carefully made, proper wines. This wine exhibits some of the pedigree of its fancier cousins and, unfortunately, some of their priciness. Nevertheless, for a claret-lover intolerant of compromise and with less than a tenner in his pocket, this wine will prove typically appealing.

Médoc AC 1987   12   £C

Mercurey 1982   11   £E

Morgon 1989   14   £D
In spite of the price, a beaujolais cru from Georges Duboeuf of real depth and flavour. Drink chilled or drink in three or four years' time – this wine is versatile with an immediate gamy fruitiness yet woody complexity hinting at its ageing potential. A handsome wine.

St-Emilion AC 1986   12   £C

St-Julien 1986   13   £E

FRENCH WINE – *white*

Beau Mont de Gras, Côtes du Viverais 1990   15   £B
Marvellously clean, delicately fruity, with a good balance of
acidity. A brilliant little wine, basically a Côtes du Rhône,
made by a Frenchman who's obviously picked up a lot of
good ideas from New World wine-makers and coaxed a
degree of distinction from the marsanne and clairette
grape varieties. These grapes all come from fifteen growers
in the commune of St Remeze in the Ardèche. The wine is
an excellent aperitif as well as being good with food like
fish and chicken dishes, even those with fancy sauces. It
has a good bit of body and the right touch of richness to
stay the course. The labelling is as elegant and purposeful
as the wine in the bottle of which, alas, only 4000 cases (of
the 1990) were made. Outstanding value for money.

Beaujolais Blanc 1988   13   £C
Not an aligoté but a chardonnay. Nevertheless the wine
has the freshness beaujolais blanc usually exhibits. A well-
made wine of some style.

Blush   12   £B
Fruity charm complemented by its pretty colour, marred
only by its awful name which sounds like the *nom de danse*
of the least talented of a Folies Bergères line-up.

Bouches du Rhône   11   £A

Burgundy AC 1989   12   £C

Chablis AC 1989   13   £D
Available in half-bottles also.

Chablis Premier Cru Beauroy 1987   16   £E

This is a very expensive white wine, but if you want to experience what a beautifully structured, pedigree beast chardonnay can be, then this chablis is it. It is superb in its fruity greenness yet restrained, elegant richness, and better than many a raddled meursault at loads more money. It is a fine wine of grassy/lemony aroma and what wine writers are pleased to call clean fruit – which means there is nary a trace of those tainting chemicals or the sweaty intrusion of syrup.

Chardonnay   14   £C

This has a typical farmyardy chardonnay pong and an uncomplicated, fruity taste. Very good value.

Chardonnay de Chardonnay 1989   13   £C

You can't get a more authentic chardonnay than this – it comes from the village near Mâcon which gives the grape its name. And a good clean wine, with a gentle touch of fruit, it is.

Château de Poce 1990   12   £C

Château de Poce is an orphanage, according to M & S, which produces chenin grapes for a local vigneron to turn into this rich, almost creamy, rounded wine which is very good for drinks parties where you have a myriad of palates to tickle and all manner of sticky things to nibble.

Cheverny 1990   13   £B

Made from a grape no one has heard of (the romorantin), this underdog appeals to me immediately. The wine is clean and dry, with a curious bready softness all its own.

Côtes de Gascogne 1990   13   £B

Very good value – dry, freshly fruity (not tinned), and harmoniously acidic.

Côtes de St-Mont 1989   14   £B

No vast claims can be made for the bouquet, it merely gets
on with politely hinting at its degree of fruitiness, but in
taste and body it has some meat, some steel and some
character which combine to make up for the initial aromatic lack. Pleasant as an aperitif but more at home when a
dozen empty bellies turn up for lunch and that school of
mackerel you have in the fridge ends up under the grill and
this wine is served with them.

Domaine de Pradelles, Gaillac 1990   14   £B

This wine is made by a well-known friend of the British
supermarket wine buyer, a *cave co-opérative* in Gaillac
called Labastide de Levis (where, for instance, the
Sainsbury's wine buyers get their Gaillac from). This
Gaillac, however, is the mellowest I've ever tasted. It's a
very individual style, for one thing, with subtle, musty, ripe
melon overtones to the typical Gaillac cleanness. This
individuality is not surprising, however, for the wine,
though vinified by the co-op's wine-maker Marie-Paule
Colombie, is from a single estate run by the Cahuzac
family, who are patently keen to deliver only first-class
grapes. These grape varieties provide further clues to the
wine's particular individuality and also evidence of the
trouble the Cahuzac family go to as vignerons; for these
varieties are the mauzac and the loin de l'oeil – this latter,
translating as 'far from the eye', rejoicing in its name
because the grape bunch grows in a curious fashion,
developing not close to the eye as normal but further along.
One result of this singular growth pattern is that the grapes
are useless if picked merely ripe, they have to be very ripe,
indeed almost decayed. This gives the wine a pleasing
vegetal fruit aroma and taste. A remarkable wine, in fact,

because it demonstrates that when the French put themselves out they can produce the best white wine in the
world for the money and do it from under-rated areas and
unfashionable grapes. Though they will need more than
just this marvellous example's output to take over the
world, as so few bottles have been made. If word gets
around it will sell out in a day.

Fleur de Rosé 13 £B
A marvellous exercise in both marketing and oenology
from Georges Duboeuf: elegant bottle and label, engaging
colour and a level of fruitiness which makes the wine floral
and yet dry, enabling it to be drunk really cold, as good
rosés should be, without the fullness being masked.

French Country 10 £B

French Dry White Anjou 13 £C
Good value and good clean fun. A happy blend of chenin
and sauvignon grape varieties. Ideal for lots of people at a
fish supper.

French Medium White 12 £B

Jean Louis Chancel, Vin de Pays de Vaucluse
1990 13 £B
On and off over the years, I've spent some time in Pertuis
in Provence, where this wine comes from, but I had to
travel to a wine-tasting at the M & S head office in
London's Baker Street before I discovered a white wine
from there which I can truly say is enjoyable.

Jeunes Vignes 14 £C
A really delicious, green-grassy, delicately fruity chablis-
in-the-making. It has subtle qualities which need some
catching, but the charm is all there in spite of the wine

being made from vines too immature to permit their vinified progeny to be termed chablis. A lovely zesty twist in
the tail as the wine leaves the throat. Better value than ever
in these perilously pricey times.

Mâcon Villages 1989   12   £D

Meursault, Les Bouchères 1987   10   £G
A lot of loot for a lot of snoot (i.e. fancy price, fancy name).
But do you really get a wine five times as good as one of
M & S's little £3 glories? I fancy not. True, you get some
bouquet, and some weight of matured oaky fruit, but,
goodness, what a price to pay.

Muscat de Beaumes de Venise AC 1987   15   £D
The dollop of honey and toasted almonds is the Beaumes
de Venise trademark. A superb dessert wine in the clinging
mould.

Pinot Grigio 1989   11   £B
A bit rounded, almost sweetish, for my taste. Unusual.
M & S say it is 'an alternative style' of the pinot grigio
grape.

Pinot Gris 1988   11   £C
A touch of treacle I fancy I found in this wine. Serendipity
from the highly rated Pfaffenheim co-operative in Alsace.

Pouilly-Fuissé 1987   12   £E

Rosé d'Anjou   12   £C

Sancerre, La Charmette 1989   12   £D

Sauvignon   11   £B

GERMAN WINE – *white*

Bereich Nierstein 1989	11	£B
Hock (1 litre)	11	£B
Liebfraumilch	10	£B
Moselle (1 litre)	11	£C
Piesporter Michelsberg 1989	12	£C

ITALIAN WINE – *red*

Bardolino 1990   14   £B
If you want to taste what the lucky residents of Lake Garda enjoy with an early-evening supper, then try this wine. It is light cherry in hue and flavour, with the suggestion of sesame biscuit, and it is simply delicious, especially chilled, at any time of the year. Makes a terrific aperitif nicely cold, and it is good with salads and antipasto.

Brunello di Montalcino 1980   14   £E
A well-matured wine to be taken seriously, being no care-free, open-necked fruitcake on a Vespa; rather, a double-breasted solid citizen in a Mercedes. As such, with its fruit spread chewily on a thin biscuit of acidity, this is a wine for well-ripened cheeses or sumptuous roasts.

Chianti Villa Cafaggio 1986   14   £D
This has the characteristic Tuscan terracotta taste of the sangiovese grape neatly held in an earthy grip. Bloody good stuff.

Italian Table Wine (1 litre)	10 £B

Settesoli Red 1989   14 £B
Like its fellow Sicilian, Settosoli Bianco, Settosoli Rosso is
a real bargain of a wine and perfect for large gatherings
and large helpings of pasta.

Valpolicella (1 litre)	12 £C

ITALIAN WINE – *white*

Chardonnay   14 £C
A well-structured wine with pretensions to class even at
this price. Dry yet firmly fruity, with that typical Italian
chardonnay 'bite', it is very good value for money. Clean.

Frascati Superiore 1989   13 £C
Pleasant clean wine with a touch of fruit. As good an
example of the house wine of Rome as you'll get.

Italian Table Wine (1 litre)   11 £B
The label speaks true; a solid and versatile party wine.

Orvieto Superiore 1989	11 £B

Settesoli White 1990   14 £B
Still holding up, this remarkable Sicilian, an excellent-
value clean white with enticing fruit, but under increasingly fierce taste and price competition from Spain.

Soave (1 litre)	10 £C

PORTUGUESE WINE – *white*

Vinho Verde 13 £B
I'm a fan of this wine. Light green by name, green by nature, unfussy, supple, very light. Very good aperitif.

SPANISH WINE – *red*

Rioja Red 13 £B
Good price for a refreshing, underrated rioja of fruity assertiveness.

Valdepenedas Red 1984 12 £B
A seven-year-old? At £3.29? What do M & S buyers do to get wine of this drinkability at this price? (Answers on a postcard please to: M & S, Baker Street, London.)

SPANISH WINE – *white*

Valdepenedas White 14 £B
A slightly insipid cucumber smell – but the ripe fruit salad taste is fantastic.

SPARKLING WINE/CHAMPAGNE

Blanc de Blancs Champagne 12 £G

Blanc de Noirs   15   £F
A champagne of great depth and style. Superb with food
due to its dry yet fruity elegance being beautifully held by a
pastry crust of flavour.

Cava   12   £C
A typical yeasty cava. Might go down well with a shellfish
stew.

Crémant d'Alsace   14   £D
Fool the champagne snobs with this one! Through aroma,
taste and finish in the throat, an excellent little fizzer.

Crémant de Bourgogne Burgundy   12/13 £D

Crémant de Bourgogne Burgundy (half)   13   £C
A good size, a stylish sparkler, not outrageous price.

Desroches   11   £F

Frizzante Moscato   10   £C

Italian Garofoli Brut NV   13   £C
A touch light, but the delicacy is fine for an aperitif. Good
value.

Nicholas Feuillatté 1982   14   £G
Quite something to find a gorgeous near-ten-year-old
champagne reclining cheek-by-jowl with a check-out
counter at my local M & S. Can it be that even the receipt
of a mere penny change out of £20 does not dispirit the
store's notoriously well-heeled impulse buyers?

Peach Royale   12   £A
Although it was described by one young worthy I offered a
glass to as 'like the syrup which surrounds tinned peaches',
I feel that at *under a quid a bottle* (and, what joy, to have

those sublime, almost metaphysically uplifting, words pass across the screen of my word processor), this wine (barely wine, forsooth, at just 5 per cent alcohol) is great very cold as an aperitif on a warm evening.

Saumur Brut 1988	12	£D

Sparkling Brut	11	£C

Sparkling Chardonnay	13	£D

Sparkling Medium Dry	12	£C

Sparkling Monmousseau 1988 14 £D
A first-class champagne substitute. Firm, not over-fruity, dry – good value.

Sparkling Rosé 14 £C
Superb little fizzer – lively, floral, fruity all the way through, yet nicely acidic. A bargain.

St-Gall 1985 12 £G
Vintage champagne at this price should be all of a piece – aroma, body, flavour and sparkle, all moving together in those tiny bubbles. This one, whilst rich and very drink-able, seems to overplay itself somewhat and have a discon-certingly incongruous fatness of taste. At its best with smoked salmon with lemon and black pepper.

Safeway

I asked a long-standing supermarket wine buyer who he thought would pick up this year's Wine Retailer of the Year Award and without a pause for breath he said 'Safeway'. Is it their turn, I asked? 'They deserve it,' he replied soberly.

Now I think it's fair to say that a few years back this exchange would have been greeted with hoots of disbelief by the wine trade and cackles of scorn by wine writers. But not today. Safeway has made massive strides and today the store is breathing hard down its competitors' necks. A competent and imaginative wine buying team, ably led, has not been content merely to pander to old-established customers' adherence to sweet sparkling wine from Italy and the treaclier concoctions from the Fatherland; the wines which were introduced during spring and summer 1991 show a variety of styles, from a spread of countries, characterized by easy drinking and value for money.

A couple of Yugoslavian reds exemplify these admirable virtues splendidly. As do half a dozen attractive Italian whites and some soft reds from the Rhône. Chile puts in an appearance and, though far from cheap, California stars in the voluptuous shape of one of my favourite pinot noirs, Barrow Green 1987. Australia features strongly with more than half-a-dozen excellent reds including the fabulous Taltarni 1983; better in my view than the 1988 of this wine which was voted, by a panel of experts, as one of the world's greatest, which the store also stocks.

Safeway also has several organic wines, including two of the tastiest in the form of the unpronounceable Château Caraguilhes from south west France and the truly sublime

Château Richeaume from Provence. When I quizzed a
horticultural technologist (not from Safeway) about Caraguilhes, he said that many of the claims made by vineyards
about the organic natures of their products were question-
able but that Caraguilhes, in his view, was exemplary. I
cannot comment. I go by the taste in the bottle and Caraguilhes tastes just fine to me, so I'm content to leave it at
that – although I would add that I would prefer to describe
several wines calling themselves as organic by some other
word. And the word is undrinkable. I'm glad to say that this
applies to none of the Safeway examples listed here.

Safeway also has some decent sparkling wines and
champagnes. At under a fiver a bottle, the bargain of the lot
has to be Great Western brut reserve which, though
sounding suspiciously like an Aussie theme park for lager
louts, has sufficient class in the glass to chivvy even the
most clear-headed of wedding guests into the belief that it
is champagne.

AUSTRALIAN WINE – *red*

Hardy's Classic Dry Red 1990   14   £C
Around £3.50, this is excellent value. Apart from the tell-
ing spiciness (which is subtle), the wine would pass, with
its handsome blend of cabernet sauvignon and shiraz, as
some oldish bordeaux of some far from minor château.

Jacob's Creek Dry Red 1988   13   £B

Orlando RF Cabernet Sauvignon 1987   13   £C

**Penfold's Bin 222, Eden Valley Cabernet
Sauvignon 1985**   14   £E

| Penfold's Bin 28, Kalimna Shiraz 1987 | 13 | £C |

| Penfold's Bin No 2, Shiraz/Mataro 1989, Barossa Valley | 12 | £C |

| Rosemount Cabernet Sauvignon 1988, Hunter Valley | 13 | £D |

| Semillon (Safeway) | 12 | £B |

Shiraz (Safeway)   15   £B
Fantastic value. Nice big, minty, fruity, gingery red wine.
Spicy, muscular yet light. An Oz bobby-dazzler.

**Taltarni Cabernet Sauvignon
1983, and 1988**   15(83), 13(88)   £E
Extraordinary full, rich wine for full, rich dinner parties.
Bordeaux meets Barolo, making Taltarni a minty and softly
tannic (but not bitter) mouthful. Hugely, maturely fruity. A
great wine in all respects. But fast moving off the shelves to
be replaced by the '88 which is in the same vein but does
need more time to develop itself as brilliantly. That said,
the '88 is nevertheless an impressive wine.

AUSTRALIAN WINE – *white*

| Hardy Collection Chardonnay 1989 | 11 | £D |

| Hardy Collection Fumé Blanc 1988 | 10 | £D |

Hardy's Classic Dry White 1990   14   £B
Gorgeous hunk of fresh fruit from Aussie.

| Jacob's Creek Semillon/Chardonnay 1989 | 12 | £C |

| Orlando RF Chardonnay 1988/89 | 12 | £C |

| Plantagenet Muscat Bindoon 1989 | 13 | £D |

A light but interesting dessert wine – good with fruit tarts, but not rich ones.

| Rosemount Chardonnay 1990, Oak-Matured Hunter Valley | 13 | £D |

| Semillon/Chardonnay 1989 (Safeway) | 12 | £C |

| Wolf Blass Oak-Matured Chardonnay 1989, Bilyara Vineyards | 11 | £D |

BULGARIAN WINE – *red*

| Cabernet/Merlot Bulgarian Country Wine (Safeway) | 13 | £A |

| Plovdiv Cabernet Sauvignon 1986 | 11 | £B |

BULGARIAN WINE – *white*

| Bulgarian Country Wine (Safeway) | 12 | £A |

CHILEAN WINE – *red*

**Errazuriz Panquehue Cabernet Sauvignon
1988, Maipo**   14   £C
An interesting, velvety style of cabernet sauvignon with
healthy fruit. A bargain.

CHILEAN WINE – *white*

Valdezaro Sauvignon Blanc   11   £B

FRENCH WINE – *red*

Beaujolais (Safeway)	11	£C
Beaujolais Villages 1989 (Safeway)	12	£C
Cabernet Sauvignon, Vin de Pays des Coteaux de l'Ardèche (Safeway)	13	£B
Château Brondelle 1988	12	£C
Château Canteloup 1988	13	£C
Château Castera 1989	10	£B

Château de Caraguilhes 1989, Corbières   14   £C
The new breed of Corbières-makers are setting a fine
example with their reds. This organic representative is one
of the best – a deep red, with surprising complexity to its
aroma and distinct strata to its fruitiness. One of those

organic wines you feel you can actually sense was grown in rich dark earth.

Château Jalette 1989	13	£B

Château Jalette 1990	11	£B

Château Joanny 1989, Côtes du Rhône 14 £B
Grass, herbs and fruit at a fair price.

Château Julien 1989, Minervois (Safeway) 13 £B
Dark, intense colour, biscuity fruit. The wine embraces the teeth in a very pleasant tannic and vegetal grip which is nothing if not friendly.

Château Les Confréries 1989, Bordeaux 13 £B
A serious bordeaux at a bargain price – good stalky fruit.

Château Les Confréries 1990	12	£B

Château Mendoce 1989	10	£C

Châteauneuf-du-Pape, La Source aux Nymphes 1988 13 £D

Corbières (Safeway)	10	£B

Côtes du Rhône (Safeway)	12	£B

Côtes du Roussillon Villages 1988 (Safeway) 12 £B
Not much in the way of smell, but agreeable plonky fruit.

Côtes de Ventoux (Safeway)	11	£B

Domaine Anthéa 1990, Merlot, Vin de Pays d'Oc No rating £B
By press date I hadn't tasted this 1990, but previous vintages of this organic wine were marvellous, and eyebrow-raising value for money. I loved it for the sheer colour and

thrill of the organic, fruity taste. Try it and let me know what you think.

Domaine de Picheral, Cépage Syrah 1989, Vin de Pays d'Oc   12   £B

Interesting how an organic wine-producer contrived to persuade grapes to taste of petrol and made the experience enjoyable.

Domaine des Cabannes 1988, Côtes du Frontonnais   10   £B

Domaine des Salaises 1988   15   £C

Usually Loire reds like this sport more of the local red wine grape (cabernet franc) in their make-up than any other; but this one has more cabernet sauvignon, the prize specimen of Bordeaux. The result, however, is not at all like the country cousin having elocution lessons and trying to pass as something it is not. The grower's technique and, more especially, the northern soil, cannot disguise this wine's provenance, whatever the predominant grape variety; therefore you will not be surprised at its black-boardy fruity taste and dry, chewy edge. Open a couple of hours before you want to drink it, and also chill it.

Domaine des Salaises 1989, Saumur (Safeway)   13   £C

Domaine la Tuque Bel-Air 1986   13   £C

Domaine Richeaume 1989   17   £E

The strongest argument yet constructed for the advantages of organic wine. This absolute stunner, a cabernet sauvignon from Provence, is not at all expensive for its exquisite tannin and fruit balance. It is a perfect wine of its kind – i.e. it is difficult to imagine anyone in the province making

such a profoundly exciting wine. I drank it with roast quail
and framboise sauce and I would have happily been taken
out and shot afterwards. The wine coats the teeth lovingly
with dry fruit and then delivers a lengthy finish of rich
sweet blackcurrant. No bottle created more happiness for
me than this one during the whole writing of *Superplonk*
1992.

French Organic Vin de Table (Safeway)	11	£B
Gévrey Chambertin, Laboure-Roi 1988	10	£F
Médoc (Safeway)	11	£C
Minervois (Safeway)	12	£A
Oak-Aged Claret 1987 (Safeway)	12	£C
St-Emilion (Safeway)	12	£C
Syrah, Vin de Pays des Coteaux de l'Ardèche (Safeway)	12	£B
Vin de Pays Catalan (Safeway)	11	£A
Vin de Pays de l'Ardèche 1990 (Safeway) Good value for money.	13	£A
Vin de Pays de la Cité de Carcassonne (Safeway)	13	£A

FRENCH WINE – *white*

Anjou Blanc (Safeway)	13	£B
Bordeaux Blanc Medium Dry (Safeway)	10	£B

Cabernet d'Anjou	10	£B

Chardonnay 1989, Bourgogne, Caves de Mancey 11 £C

Chardonnay, Vin de Pays des Coteaux de l'Ardèche 1989 11 £C

Château Bastor Lamontagne 1989, Sauternes (half) 14 £C
Marvellous half-bottle. Jammy, rich and curranty with enough honey to send Pooh Bear aloft.

Château Canet 1990, Entre-Deux-Mers 11 £C
Organic.

Château de la Botinière 1990, Muscadet de Sèvre-et-Maine Sur Lie 13 £C

Château l'Oiseau 1990, Entre-Deux-Mers (Safeway) 12 £B

Château les Combes 1990, Bordeaux 11 £B

Corbières Blanc de Blancs 1990 (Safeway) 12 £B

Côtes du Lubéron 1990 (Safeway) 11 £E

Graves Sec (Safeway) 12 £B

Meursault 1988, Laboure-Roi (Safeway) 8 £F

Muscat, Cuvée José Sala 16 £B
Luscious honeyed, nougaty stuff which by only one penny nudges into the B-price band. It is, then, startlingly wonderful value. It also nudges your taste-buds into paradise if you have the right dessert with it – fruit meringue, for instance.

Pinot Blanc d'Alsace 1990	12	£C
Riesling d'Alsace 'Woelfelin' 1989	13	£B
Sancerre Domaine de Petits Perriers 1990	10	£E
Sauvignon, Cuvée Ramond, 1990	13	£B
Sauvignon de Haut Poitou 1990 VDQS	12	£C

Viognier 1991   No rating   £C

This is unrated because this vintage, if it comes up to
scratch, will not be on sale until early 1992 and I have yet
to swig it. But the wine is so interesting, and the 1990 I
tasted so appealing, that it is worth bringing to your attention. I rated the 1990 15 points for its outstanding creamy
softness, rather like a Châteauneuf-du-Pape blanc, and
elegant dry apricot structure. At under £4 it is a beautiful
bargain. Viognier is one of the world's greatest grapes but
also one of the least grown – until recently it blossomed
in only a few dozen acres of the Rhône. This example,
from the Ardèche (the Italians and Californians are also
beginning to make wine from the grape), is worth looking
out for. And worth every penny. I hope for your sake – and
mine, since I shall buy several cases – Safeway decide to
stock it. This is not absolutely certain at the time of going
to press. Keep your fingers crossed.

Vouvray Demi Sec   10   £C

GERMAN WINE – *white*

| **Bereich Bernkastel, Mosel-Saar-Ruwer (Safeway)** | 12 | £B |

Flonheimer Adelberg Kerner Spätlese 1988, Rheinhessen 12 £D
Organic.

Gewürztraminer Rheinpfalz Halbtrocken (Safeway) 10 £C

Hock, Deutscher Tafelwein (Safeway) 10 £A
Give a glass to Gran (or to the cat for Christmas).

Morio-Muskat 1990, St Ursula 12 £B

Reiler Mullay-Hofberg Riesling Auslese 1988 12 £D
Nice touch of seaweed on the finish. Good aperitif.

Riesling Rheinhessen (Safeway) 12 £B

Rulander Kabinett 1988, Ihringer Winklerberg 12 £C

St-Ursula Kerner 1990, Rheinhessen 13 £C
Quite delicious. A lovely organic aperitif.

Trierer Deutschherrenberg Riesling Spätlese 1983 11 £D

Trocken Silvaner 1988, Ihringer Vulkanfelsen 11 £B

Zeltinger Himmelreich Riesling Kabinett 1989 10 £C

HUNGARIAN WINE – *red*

Merlot, Villany Region (Safeway)   13   £A
Usual excellent merlot – soft, fruity, attractive and very
good value for money.

HUNGARIAN WINE – *white*

Dry Muscat, Nagyrede   12   £A

ISRAELI WINE – *red*

**Carmel Cabernet Sauvignon Samsom Region
(Kosher)**   12   £C
An interesting curiosity; dry and respectably clothed in
fruit.

ISRAELI WINE – *white*

**Carmel Riesling, Samson Region (Kosher)
Medium Dry**   10   £C

ITALIAN WINE – *red*

Bardolino (Safeway)	13	£B
Chianti (Safeway)	13	£B

Chianti Classico 1986, Rocca delle Macie   13   £C
A good, firm, well-aged chianti at a good price.

Nebbiolo del Piemonte 1986 (Safeway)   12   £D
An enthralling curiosity, this barrel-aged northerner. It's
as brown as old boots but very sweet-natured and fruity to
the point of Christmas pudding-curranty richness. Great
with smelly cheese and might be interesting with game.
But very expensive.

Terrale 1990   14   £B
Full ripe taste with lively fruitiness. Terrific value from
Sicily.

Valpolicella Classico 1988 'Vigneti Marano'   14   £C
Lovely light wine. Striking balance of acid and fruit makes
it good to chill, like a beaujolais, to enjoy with salads and
charcuterie.

Valpolicella (Safeway)   12   £B

ITALIAN WINE – *white*

Chardonnay del Triveneto 1990, Vino da Tavola
(Safeway)   13   £C

Fontana Candida Frascati Superiore Secco
1988   10   £C

Orvieto Classico Secco 1990 (Safeway)   12   £B

Pinot Grigio del Triveneto 1990, Vino da
Tavola (Safeway)   13   £B

Sauvignon del Triveneto 1990 (Safeway)   14   £B
Excellent fruit/acid harmony – lovely melony/lemon edge.
Very clean. Excellent.

Soave (Safeway)   10   £B

Terrale 1990   15   £B
Voluptuous madonna of a wine. The fruit is all bosom, the
acid languid and fresh, and what soul there is is pure
devil-driven. Glorious cheap plonk. Must be the house red
of every whore-house in Sicily.

Verdicchio delle Marche 1990, Vino da Tavola
(Safeway)   12   £B

NEW ZEALAND WINE – *white*

Montana Sauvignon Blanc 1990, Marlborough, South
Island   11   £C

Nobilo 'White Cloud' Müller-Thurgau 1990,
Gisborne, North Island   12   £C
An excellent aperitif wine.

ROMANIAN WINE – *white*

Tamaioasa Pietroasele 1986   13 £C
An interesting touch of stale cabbage (or is it the socks
worn by the grape-pressers?) with the fruit. Worthy, elegant wine for creamy, fruity puds.

SPANISH WINE – *red*

Cariñena 1987 (Safeway)   10 £B

Don Darias   12 £B
The vanilla cries out: 'Food! Food! In heaven's name –
food!'

Don Darias Bodegas Vitorianas   12 £A

Navajas 1985   13 £C
Pleasant light stuff, under-oaked and civilized company for
what is traditionally an old sweat-bag of a wine.

Raimat Merlot 1988, Costers del Segre   11 £D

Raimat Tempranillo 1988, Costers del Segre 14 £D
A lovely toasted, fruity wine but, like the name says, it
costers.

Rioja Crianza 1987   12 £C

Viña Pedrosa 1986, Ribera del Duero   13 £C
This wine rates 17 for smoothness, 12 for aroma, and 11
for finish. This averages 13.

SPANISH WINE – *white*

Casa Lo Alto 1989, Utiel Requeña	12	£B

Penedès (Safeway)	11	£B

Rioja Rosé (Safeway) 13 £B
Nicely chilled, you will feel nicely thrilled.

Vino de Valencia Dry (Safeway) 13 £A
Outstanding value for money for a clean, dry, fruity wine
with the temerity to be almost elegant.

Zagarron 1988/89, La Mancha 11 £A

USA WINE – *red*

Barrow Green Pinot Noir 1987, California 15 £E
A stunner of a pinot noir. Enough to make many of the
wine-makers of the Côte d'Or pack up, go home and
retire, and contemplate less competitive pursuits. Has
everything the lover of this style of wine could wish for –
calm, gamy fruit, lush acidity, satin texture.

**Christian Brothers Napa Valley Cabernet
Sauvignon 1986** 13 £D

Geoffrey Roberts California Red 10 £B

**Quady Elysium Black Muscat 1989,
California (half)** 10 £D
This exaggerated style shows cinnamon and cloves and
blackberry jam. A curiosity to drink with God knows what.

USA WINE – *white*

Californian White (Safeway)	10	£A

Geoffrey Roberts California White   12   £B
It doesn't seem possible for a wine to be made in California and end up on our dinner tables at under three quid. This wine is worth its trip and shows no fatigue from the long journey.

YUGOSLAVIAN WINE – *red*

Milion Pinot Noir 1988, Vranje   15   £A
A delicious light pinot noir with a vegetal biscuity fruitiness. Fantastic value for money.

YUGOSLAVIAN WINE – *white*

Laski Rizling (Safeway)	12	£C

SPARKLING WINE/CHAMPAGNE

Albert Etienne Brut 1985 (Safeway)	12	£G
Albert Etienne Rosé Brut (Safeway)	12	£G
Albert Etienne (Safeway)	13	£F

Chardonnay Spumante (Safeway)   13   £D
Very pleasant champagne substitute.

Codorniu Blanc de Blancs 1987, Cava   14   £E
Superbly elegant fizzer. A real find. Has to be bought
instead of champagne. A bargain at this price.

**Codorniu Première Cuvée 1989, Cava
(magnum)**   12   £F
Buy it for the elegance, the style and the big fat magnum.

**Crémant de Bourgogne Blanc de Blancs
(Safeway)**   13   £D

**Great Western Brut Reserve, South
Australia**   15   £D
A bargain champagne in all but name (and what does that
count for nowadays?)

La Sirena Cava Brut   12   £C

Sparkling Blackcurrant   15   £B
This is pure unadulterated blackcurrant in smell and taste.
This is not surprising since no grape gets a look in, just
blackcurrants. It is great fun and a hilarious addition to a
party or to a Christmas lunch.

Sparkling Strawberry   16   £B

Vin Mousseux Brut (Safeway)   11   £B

Vouvray Tête de Cuvée Brut   12   £D

Sainsbury's

Accompanying a pair of Sainsbury wine buyers on a buying trip to the south of France last autumn, I was treated to a rare insight into the store and into the life of the professional wine buyer. Wine, you might think, is a doddle to buy. You take off somewhere warm, swill oodles of free booze some of which you like, and you sign a purchase order – oh, and the grateful vineyard owners treat you to lots of satisfying and hugely filling lunches and dinners. Only this last is true and, if my experience is anything to go by, 'hugely filling' is an understatement. I was so stuffed with hospitality by the end of the second day I was begging to go home. How did the buyers put up with it? It was freezing cold (September in open vineyards in Bordeaux and Toulouse being nothing like September on open beaches in Cannes), we tasted masses of wines we didn't like, and the nearest an order got to being placed was when one of the buyers said, after tasting scores of wines over several days, 'We quite like this one. Send some further samples to London and we'll see how it travels.' Did the eager wine-makers appear miffed? Not a bit of it. They enthusiastically pressed upon us further examples of their treasured liquids – red, white, rosé and, in one extraordinary instance, bright yellow with green glints – and my palate felt like a well-used playing field upon which unsympathetic studded boots had unkindly trodden. True, the wine-makers also fortified us with truffled wild mushrooms, chickens, pigeons, fois gras, fresh river fish, homemade noodles, and rare vintages from their areas (in one never-to-be-forgotten moment, the fruits of a recent and spectacular gallstone operation was pressed upon me for inspection in the middle of dinner *en famille*) but the trip was never less than commercial and the pace never less than purposeful and hectic.

As is the existence of the wine-makers themselves. Finding yourself in the position of supplying Sainsbury's may be good business but it is also nerve-racking. The grower's life is fraught with the unexpected; for though the store's buyers may make appointments weeks beforehand, not so the technologists. These inquisitive and demanding individuals thrive on catching growers off guard; not giving them an opportunity to sweep the bottling plant floor or repair that mistiming valve, let alone to lay out the red carpet, beforehand. Yet were such technical faults to be discovered on a surprise visit, the wine-maker would be in trouble; he could even lose his or her contract to supply. Is this resented? Apparently not; even when it hurts that object closest to a Frenchman's heart, his wallet. Indeed, it was a cheerful co-operative wine-maker who told me that due to Sainsbury's technologists his co-op had to shell out seven million francs on new plant. 'On the bottling line mostly,' he added.

It was the same story at another supplier who has a sizeable operation near Bordeaux. 'Sainsbury's inspectors have been of tremendous help to us in technical respects,' I was told by managing director Jean-François Mau as we stood looking at his bottling plant the morning after the dinner at which his father had served up his gallstones. We stared at the bottles as they proceeded hugger-mugger along the line, passing out of the capsuling apparatus like a never-ending queue of cowled Benedictines departing chapel. 'Two-and-a-half million bottles a year,' said Jean-François proudly. These include, as far as Sainsbury's is

concerned (for Mau supplies other British supermarkets), a
Côtes de Castillon called Manoir du Gravoux, the store's
own-label Médoc, and a Bergerac blanc. Good wines all.

'What, however, apart from the quality of the wines, does
Sainsbury's look for in a supplier like this?' I asked one of
the buyers.

'We're after consistency of supply and sufficient moder-
nity to ensure a clean and reliable product. And all at a price
we can do business at.'

The other buyer chipped in. 'We also look for kindred
spirits,' he said.

This last remark is revealing. What place has a 'kindred
spirit' in the tough business world of mass-market produce
buying? Or is it a Sainsbury's peculiarity, a weakness, the
cynic might say, to seek such ineffable rapport between
buyer and producer?

I suppose the answer has to do with the fact that regular
Sainsbury's customers do more than buy the slogan 'Where
good food costs less'. They buy the store's ethos. The
loyalty this ethos creates is not so far removed from that
which, when I was a kid, my mother had in Mr Patterson our
local grocer; at Sainsbury's, many shoppers seem to believe,
they have found a kindred spirit. This is exactly the same
feeling expressed by that Sainsbury's buyer.

And it has everything to do with one individual's belief in
another. At the biggest and most commercial winery I
visited on my Sainsbury's trip, I was given the most convinc-
ing evidence of this.

'Our vignerons know perfectly well that they are growing
grapes to make wine to be sold in Sainsbury's supermarkets,' said the technical director to me. 'But what they
really want to believe is that they are helping to make wine
which is bought and enjoyed by Lord Sainsbury himself.'

AUSTRALIAN WINE – *red*

Cook's Cabernet/Merlot 1988   12   £C
Lay it down for a couple of years. Dry and dusty (cabernet
dominating over the merlot), but it will improve.

AUSTRALIAN WINE – *white*

Chenin Semillon (Sainsbury's)   12   £B

Jacob's Creek Semillon/Chardonnay 1990   12   £C

**Mitchelton Botrytis Affected Rhine Riesling
1983**   10   £C
At 11.5 per cent alcohol, not enough power for a dessert
wine.

Mitchelton Marsanne 1988   11   £D

Rhine Riesling (Sainsbury's)   10   £B

Rothbury Chardonnay 1989   14   £D
Elegant and fruity, but not fruit of the tinned variety. Nice
lemon (but not acidic) finish.

AUSTRIAN WINE – *white*

Bouvier Trockenbeerenauslese 1989   13   £D
Not as pungent as its German counterpart. It ought to be
aged more to develop its undoubted complex character.

Still, if you're feeling extravagant, and someone's given you a pound of strawberries, treat yourself.

BULGARIAN WINE – *red*

Bulgarian Cabernet Sauvignon (Sainsbury's) 13 £B

Stambolovo Merlot Special Reserve 1985 10 £D
Drinkable enough, to be sure, but not a fiver's worth of fruit by a long chalk.

BULGARIAN WINE – *white*

Welsch-Riesling (Sainsbury's) (3-litre box) 14 £E
Welsch-Riesling is a grape grown near the banks of the Danube, and it makes a clean yet rounded wine, rather in the chardonnay mould but without the layers of flavour. The box is great value for parties or to keep in the fridge when you fancy the odd glass.

CHILEAN WINE – *red*

Chilean Cabernet Sauvignon 14 £B
Most approachable soft cabernet with gentle aromatics, handsome soft fruit and good manners on the finish. Bargain wine.

CHILEAN WINE – *white*

Chilean Sauvignon Blanc   14   £B
Delicate, clean, perfectly weighted fruit, not sharp. Good
value.

Santa Rita Chardonnay 1990   13   £D
Impressive, but not cheap.

CHINESE WINE – *white*

Tsingtao Chinese Chardonnay 1987   12   £C
Not a bad wine if you like oodles of canned fruit on the
nose in the Australian style. This wine is made by an
Australian, who supervises wine-making at this Chinese
vineyard. At this price, however, it has stiff competition.
Interesting curiosity, though.

FRENCH WINE – *red*

Anjou Rouge (Sainsbury's)   12   £B

**Beaujolais-Villages, Château des Vergers
1989**   8   £C
So, even the winners of the last two years' 'Supermarket
Wine Merchant of the Year Award' can't get it right all of
the time.

Bergerac Rouge (Sainsbury's)   12   £B

**Bergerie de l'Arbous Coteaux de Languedoc
1988** 13 £C

Bourgueil, Domaine des Forges 1986 12 £D
Good to find a Loire red with this amount of bottle age on
a supermarket shelf, but, curiously, this example, in
acquiring its age, has lost some of the distinctive lead-
pencil fruitiness of the type.

**Cabardes 1987, Château de Pennautier
(Sainsbury's)** 14 £B
Terrific bargain. Richly edged, dry yet rounded, this wine
is a very attractive mouthful.

Cabernet Sauvignon, Selection Skalli 14 £B
Excellent value – elegant, mature, fruity yet dry.

Cahors, Château Les Bouysses 1987 12 £C
Subdued fruit, chewy wine. Craggy and coarse but a genuine character. Smashing with cheese – the acidity of the
wine tackles it beautifully.

**Château Arnaud, Haut-Médoc, 1987
(1.5 litres)** 13 £F
Very dryish fruit. Good partner for all roast meats.

Château Artigues Arnaud 1988, Pauillac 13 £D
Second wine of Grand Puy Ducasse. Lay it down for at
least a year (I wrote in April '91), so the tannin grip softens
more. Good now but not especially complex – it's a bit like
a piano piece played only on the white keys.

Château Barreyres, Haut-Médoc 1988 14 £D
The bitter fruit is well harnessed by the aroma. A very
good-value wine for the seriousness of the style.

Château Bellevue la Forêt 1989   14 £B
Stalky and aromatic, rather sternly made, but this disappears with roasts.

Château Blaignan, Médoc 1986 (1.5 litres)   14 £F
Distinguished, biscuity, fruity flavour – distinct blackberry nose. Elegant. Some finesse. Love the big bottle.

Château Cantemerle, Haut-Médoc 1987   12 £G

Château Croix des Lauriers 1986, Bordeaux 15 £B
Easily the most impressively styled claret for under £3.50 I've tasted for a while. Serious wine of depth, richness and some muscularity with the fruit.

Château Dauzac, Margaux 1985   13 £F

**Château de Gallifet, Cairanne 1988, Côtes du
Rhone Villages**   14 £C
Terrific dry-edged fruitiness makes this a handsome wine. Good price for such sophisticated drinking.

Château de Pizay, Morgon 1988   12 £D

Château Grand-Puy Ducasse, Pauillac 1987 12 £E
Take it easy for a few years, *vieux sport*, and we'll see how you turn out.

Château La Vieille Cure, Fronsac 1987   14 £D
Elegance, class and calm manners. Posh dinner-party wine, but easy to drink all the same. Not over-serious.

Château La Vieille Cure 1987   15 £D
This is an instantly likeable bordeaux at a bargain price for such classy tippling. Bouquet: blackcurrant on a bed of cedar wood. Taste: crumpled satin. Finish in the throat: softness and richness. The store says the wine 'has a long

youthful finish' – a phrase they must have borrowed from one of the calling cards which certain ladies in my area of London are given to papering phone boxes with; this may, or may not, give you a clue to the wine's ready sensuality.

Château Léoville Barton 1987, St-Julien   14   £F
Treacly-rich and open. Very warm drinking.

Château les Bouysses, Cahors 1987   13   £C
A rich, dark wine with an agreeable chewiness, making it excellent news for rich dark stews.

Château Maucaillou, Moulis 1986   14   £F
A real classy wine in terms of fruit, finesse and serious dryness of character.

Château Rozier 1986, St-Emilion Grand Cru   14   £E
Delicious, calm, smelly and fruity. Oaky and vegetal, yet fruitily dry. Very cosy soft wine of some distinction. Class act. Mature. Not as friendly as some – demands that attention and respect are paid to it. Won't let you get away with a hasty slurp, you have to think about it. (So reads my tasting note.)

Château Tourteau-Chollet, Graves 1986   13   £D
This has elegance and class: dry fruit, not overloaded or tannic. A touch of burnt wood on the finish.

Claret Bordeaux Supérieur (Sainsbury's)   14   £B
This must be among the best-value wines that claret lovers can get their hands on, since it is nothing more nor less than a cabernet sauvignon of simple construction yet undeniable pedigree.

Clos du Marquis 1986, St-Julien   14   £F
Ripe melon in this one. Can't figure out how it got there.

Corbières (Sainsbury's), Château la Voulte-Gasparets 1988   16 £B
Astounding impertinence! Off with its cork! A gorgeous,
voluptuous wine of such stunning fullness and all-
embracing richness for the money you wonder if some
fellow hasn't completely screwed up the store's price-label
machine. Oooh . . . this wine is like being cuddled by Dolly
Parton.

Côtes du Rhône, Château du Prieuré 1988   11 £B

Crozes-Hermitage (Sainsbury's)   12 £C
Good value for a goodish, rich, dark, full wine of woody
fruit. Has to be drunk with food.

Domaine des Forges 1986, Bourgeuil, Cuvée les Bezards   13 £D

Domaine du Colombier Chinon 1989   15 £C
Wonderfully forward, fruity wine of immediate and seductive drinkability. Has the usual lead-pencil taste of the
cabernet franc grape, quite thrillingly softened and subtly
toffeed into glorious fruity submission. Perfect slightly
chilled, and I will confess to happily being in heaven with a
large glass of this in one hand (the rest of the bottle to
follow) and any book by V. Nabokov in the other (with the
rest of the evening to finish bottle and book in).

Fiefs de Lagrange 1987, St-Julien   15 £E
Grassy on the nose, then the richness and complexity
wallop the palate and you think, 'Good, this is an old-style
claret without tannic unfriendliness.' A very companion-
able wine with fine food: elegant, distinguished in a slightly
raffish sense, and very warmly fruity.

Fitou, les Guèches 1988 (Sainsbury's) 14 £B
What an agreeable fitou! Outstanding value at under £3
and good enough with its style to sit at any dinner party.

Hautes Côtes de Nuits, La Perrière, 1988 13 £D

Irouleguy, Domaine de Mignaberry 1988 11 £D

Le Petit Cheval, St-Emilion Grand Cru 1988 11 £G
Second wine of the legendary Château Cheval Blanc. A lot
of loot. Not a lot of boot. But drinkable. Disappointing for
the price. A well-made but ineffably dull wine; but laid
down it will improve greatly. Can you afford to wait till the
kids grow up?

Les Forts de Latour, Pauillac 1983 14 £G
Attractive forward style: gamy and fruity rather in the
manner of a velvety burgundy. The most distinguished
glassful at the tasting of second wines at which I drank it,
but it is a lot of money. It's the name you're paying for;
Forts de Latour is not Château Latour but another wine,
from a separate stretch of vines, made by the same people
– hence its designation 'second wine'. If you want the
name Latour on your dinner table, however, then you'll
have pay for it.

Marsannay 1987, Chenu 14 £D
A highly drinkable, very good burgundy. Will improve if
cellared for some years. Very good value.

Mondot 1988, St-Emilion 15 £E
A real meaty rotweiler of a wine – grabs you and won't let
go. Husky voice of fruit and rich berries. A wonderful wine
with food – it lives for it!

Nuits St-Georges, Clos de Thorey 1985 12 £G

Pavillon Rouge du Château Margaux 1988   14   £G
Rose-water, blackcurrants and ripe figs – elegance, fullness, distinction.

Red Burgundy, Pinot Noir (Sainsbury's)   10   £C

Réserve de la Comtesse 1988, Paulliac   10   £F
Sour finish, which spoils a fair wine at a huge price.

Savigny-les-Beaune 1987   13   £E
Comforting rather than spectacular.

St-Chinian, Château Salvanhiac 1989   14   £B
What sounds like a saucy girls' school turns out to be a very properly behaved little red wine from Minervois with enough of a touch of class to its aroma, flavour, and staying power in the throat to be terrific value for money. Top-drawer style at a bargain-basement price.

**St-Emilion Grand Cru, Château Grand
Mayne 1985   14   £F**
Luscious, elegant, rich, full of flowers. Beautifully, aromatically mature. Dull finish, however – disappoints by failing to hang around for a farewell kiss. But rated 14 because of the rest of its impressive performance.

Syrah Selection Skalli   12   £B

Touraine Gamay (Sainsbury's)   12   £B

**Vin de Pays de la Cité de Carcassonne 1989,
Domaine Sautes le Bas (Sainsbury's)   12   £B**
More like mildew than merlot. Still, tastes fine with cheese, lying with sun-dried tomatoes on toast.

Vin de Pays de la Dordogne   12   £B

FRENCH WINE – *white*

Alsace Gewürztraminer 1989 (Sainsbury's)	14	£C
Alsace Pinot Blanc (Sainsbury's)	13	£C
Alsace Riesling (Sainsbury's)	12	£C
Bergerac Blanc (Sainsbury's)	13	£B
Bordeaux Sauvignon (Sainsbury's)	12	£B
Chablis 1989 (Sainsbury's)	11	£D

Chardonnay Skalli (Sainsbury's Selection)   13   £C
Good, firm, fruity, clean. And good value.

Château d'Arlay 1988   12   £E
It is impossible to rate this finely made wine from the Jura
any higher because it is so raw – it needs to nestle beside
Rip Van Winkle before it can become the outstanding
bottle which it has, I think, the potential to reach. Even
then, the taste will need to be acquired along with the
requisite ageing because the characteristics of the flavour
include iodine and green melon with a hint of sorrel.

**Château de Davenay, Montagny Premier Cru
1988**   11   £D

Château Mayne des Carmes, Sauternes 1988 15   £F
Second wine of Château Rieussec, a famed dessert wine
vineyard. Gorgeous pudding wine – honey and toffee
cobnuts and a melony, caramelly richness. Leave a glass
out for Father Christmas, along with the mince pie.

Corbières Blanc (Sainsbury's)   12   £B

Coteaux du Layon, Château du Breuil 1989   14   £D
Delightful light dessert wine for soft fruits and creamy
puds.

Côtes du Lubéron, Domaine de la Panisse 1989
(Sainsbury's)   11   £B
A respectable enough rose, but not enough round dry fruit
to give the wine that essential style when really cold. It's
this which makes a rosé such a treat if the conditions are
right.

Côtes de Provence Rosé (Sainsbury's)   11   £B

Domaine Belle Croix 1989, Coteaux de St-
Bris Bourgogne Aligoté   14   £C
This is a white burgundy good and true, but it's not a
chardonnay, it's an aligoté – a much-maligned grape
variety which has always had a friend in me. This wine is a
perfectly balanced specimen, touched by gracefulness on
the high wire of acidity, strengthed by firm, melony
richness on the low bar of fruitiness. Great stuff.

Gros Plant du Pays Nantais 1990   11   £B
Needs fresh shellfish to be at its most drinkable.

Jurançon Sec 1989 (Sainsbury's)   16   £B
I don't think Sainsbury's had great hopes for this wine at
the beginning. Since when did great dry white wine come
from the Pyrenees? But when I raved over it in a *Guardian*
article it sold out time and time again in spite of a dramatic
price rise (as a result, so I was told by the winery's agent, of
growers' costs rising). It is, simply, one of the bargains of
the decade: juicy, fruity, acidically fresh without a trace of
sharpness, and beautifully harmonized.

Le Sec de Rayne Vigneau 1990   13 £D
Lovely stylish stuff.

Meursault, Blagny 1989   15 £G
Yes, it's the real thing – albeit in a modern lighter vein.
Gently cabbagey, flowery and gamy at one and the same
time, this is a wickedly subtle wine, streaked with a delicate
balancing acidity, showing the true finesse of fine white
burgundy. If I wished to treat myself, I'd buy a bottle of
this wine, pack the kids off for the afternoon, and settle
down somewhere comfortable with a good book – Jean-
nette Winterson, for example, matches the wine's characteristics perfectly.

Mouton Cadet 1990   12 £C

Muscadet de Sèvre-et-Maine Sur Lie,
Château de la Dimerie 1990   11 £C

Muscadet de Sèvre-et-Maine Sur Lie, Domaine
Coursay-Village 1988   14 £C
This is an organic muscadet and it tastes earthily delicious.

Muscat de St-Jean de Minervois (half)   14 £B
A useful half-bottle of silky dessert wine. Especially wel-
come with tarts and puds without citric sauces.

Pouilly-Fumé les Chantalouettes 1990   11 £D

Premières Côtes de Bordeaux 1989, Domaine
Tour du Guet (Sainsbury's)   13 £C

Premières Cotes de Bordeaux NV   11 £C

Sancerre, Les Beaux Regards 1989   15 £E
The classiest sancerre on any supermarket shelf, as far as I
can judge – goosberry-fresh and clean, and deliciously dry
with a subtle melony edge.

**Vin de Pays des Côtes de Gascogne, Domaine
Bordes 1990**   14 £B
As always, clean. But enough fruit to make it a bargain.

Vin de Pays des Côtes du Tarn (Sainsbury's)   13 £B

Vin de Pays du Gers (Sainsbury's)   14 £B
Utterly delicious wine at an utterly delicious price – melons
and plums, all wrapped up whistle-clean. An outstanding
example of the new breed of wines from southern France
and, frankly, at under three quid the bottle, the New World
competition can pack up and go home – no contest.

Vin de Pays d'Oc (Sainsbury's)   13 £B
Good-value clean wine.

White Burgundy Chardonnay (Sainsbury's)   13 £C

GERMAN WINES – *white*

Alsheimer Rheinblick, Beerenauslese 1986   15 £E
Pricey, but worth it for the ortega grape's particular honeyed
style. Marvellous with any kind of pud, but especially rich
cakey ones. Liquid paradise after dinner.

Auslese Rheinpfalz 1989 (Sainsbury's)   12 £C

Baden Dry (Sainsbury's)   13 £B

**Dalsheimer Burg Rodenstein 1989
(Sainsbury's)**   14 £B
Goodness me, what a wine for under three quid! A terrific
aperitif with great acidic dash allied to herbal soft fruitiness.

Forster Mariengarten, Eugen Muller 1988   14 £C
A delightful, easy-sipping aperitif: fragrant and light.

Kabinett Rheinhessen 1989 (Sainsbury's)   14 £B
A terrific aperitif – a lovely, refreshing, acidic style cut with
undertones of herbal softness.

Kaseler Herrenberg 1988   12 £D

Morio-Muskat Rheinpfalz (Sainsbury's)   12 £B
Makes a pleasant aperitif on a hot night – as long as you
don't mind your nose in a powder compact.

Niersteiner Gutes Domtal (Sainsbury's)   11 £A

Ockfener Bockstein 1985   14 £C
Got a bit of age, this one, and it has developed into a
pleasantly rounded wine offering a bouquet of spring
flowers. Not a sweet wine at all, so makes a dandy aperitif.

Ockfener Bockstein Riesling 1985   12 £D

Riesling Nahe (Sainsbury's)   12 £B

Rivaner Rheinpfalz (Sainsbury's)   12 £B

Spätlese Mosel-Saar-Ruwer 1988
(Sainsbury's)   11 £C

Trocken Rheinhessen (Sainsbury's)   11 £B
Inoffensive aperitif providing apples and elderberry on the
nose.

GREEK WINE – *red*

Château Carras 1979   15 £C
Under a fiver, this wine is a glorious cheek of a bargain for
twelve years old. Serious, deep, herby – a delicious accompaniment for roast lamb.

GREEK WINE – *white*

Retsina   13 £B
Be honest. You see the word 'retsina' and the letters
rearrange themselves magically before your eyes to read
'nastier'. Please. Try the blighter. It's an excellent introduction to the taste of cricket bats and cheap at the price.
Handsome and, surprisingly, keenly refreshing, with the
right food. I love it.

HUNGARIAN WINE – *white*

Tokaji Aszu 5 Puttonyos 1981   13 £D
Acquired taste, this dessert wine. Old sherry meets chardonnay plus spice and salt. A small glass with dessert is a
very pleasant experience (but an acquired taste).

ITALIAN WINE – *red*

Cannonau del Parteolla (Sainsbury's)   15   £B
Cannonau is to Sardinia what garnacha is to Spain and
grenache to France and California; in the hands of the
Sardinians, the grenache becomes a lovely spicy wine of no
great complexity, just all-embracing warmth and gravelly
fruitiness.

Chianti 1990 (Sainsbury's)   12   £B

Chianti Classico 1987 (Sainsbury's)   13   £C
Classico stuff.

Dolcetto d'Aqui 1988   13   £B
Liquorice and mint covering the fruit provide the conclu-
sive evidence that this wine is a northern Italian. Very good
value. Serve with any kind of pasta and highly flavoured
dishes.

**San Lorenzo Rosso Conero 1986, Umani
Ronchi**   14   £C
A gorgeous fistful of fruit hitting the roof of the mouth –
mamma mia!

Spargolo 1985, Vino da Tavola   13   £E
Chewy, elegant, and full of itself.

Valpolicella Classico, Negarine 1989   15   £B
I adore this wine. It has taken the place that beaujolais
used to have in my affections – when that wine was both
affordable and not so rotten with sugar it was too alcoholic.
In many people's minds, valpolicella is to wine what Enid
Blyton is to literature, so this marvellous example, with its
lovely umbraceous fruity style dry-edged with digestive

biscuit, is a bargain. Please don't confuse this wine with
Sainsbury's other Valpolicella Classico below. Negarine is
the word to look for.

Valpolicella Classico (Sainsbury's) (1.5 litres)	10	£C

Vino Nobile Di Montepulciano, Fattoria di Casale 1987	13	£D

ITALIAN WINE – *white*

Avignonesi 'Il Marzocco' 1988	12	£E

**Bianco di Custoza Castel Nuova Pasqua
1990**   13   £B
A clean yet soft wine which is an admirable whistle-wetter.

Casal di Serra, Verdicchio dei Castelli Jesi   14   £B
Seriously good drinking at a cheap price: nutty, fresh,
ever-so-gently citric, and so elegantly assertive.

Casato delle Macie 1989   13   £C
Here, the immigrant chardonnay has a lovely fattening
effect on the native trebbiano grape and, rather like a decent
Chinese restaurant arriving in an English high street, provides a healthy dash of exotica. The wine is quite delicious.

Chardonnay Alto Adige 1989 (Sainsbury's)   15   £C
This area, and this particular maker, is producing some
truly terrific chardonnays of which this example is exceptional in both flavour and price. The wine has all the
restrained, elegant fruitiness to be expected of well-made
chardonnay plus a dash of Italian bravura; this makes it a

wine to be relished by itself or enjoyed with foods as strongly flavoured as *pollo sorpresa* or *zuppa di pesce*.

Chardonnay del Piemonte 1990	13	£B

Chardonnay, Zenato 1989   13   £C

Cortese alto Monferrato 1990   13   £B
Elegant, very elegant.

Gavi, Bersano 1990   13   £C

Moscato d'Asti, Vecchio Piemonte   10   £B

Pinot Grigio, Grave del Friuli Collavini 1990   12   £C
Delicious in its own way, but I wonder if the label provides more of a talking-point than the wine in the bottle? Perilously close to a fiver a bottle for comfort.

Soave Classico Costalunga, Pasqua 1989
(Sainsbury's)   11   £B

Trebbiano di Romagna (Sainsbury's)
(1.5 litres)   13   £C

Verduzzo del Piave (Sainsbury's)   14   £B
This is an outstanding bargain. Dry but not bony, fruity but not brassy.

Vermentino di Sardegna (Sainsbury's)   14   £B
A very stylish Sardinian: on the dry side of rounded with soft fruit undertones. Good with grilled fish. Excellent value for money.

Vernaccia di San Gimignano 1989, San
Quirico   13   £C
A terrific wine with shellfish; dry, gentle, fruity and not overfull of itself.

LEBANESE WINE – *red*

Château Musar 1982   17 £D
The magical wine of the Lebanon. (See Asda for more
details.)

NEW ZEALAND WINE – *red*

Cook's Cabernet/Merlot 1988   11 £C
Well, yes, cooks might find the wine useful for marinades,
but I find it drinkable though oddly unharmonious – being
both green and over-ripe at the same time. This is a
remarkable vinous attribute, and it may be that the cabernet sauvignon (65 per cent) and merlot (35 per cent) grape
varieties, being vinified separately and then blended, are
still engaged and holding hands rather than married and in
bed together. Perhaps a few more months in bottle, in the
warm congenial atmosphere of your local Sainsbury's, may
bring the wine around.

NEW ZEALAND WINE – *white*

Cook's Hawkes Bay, Sauvignon Blanc 1989   12 £C

Craigmoor Chardonnay 1988   11 £C

Nobilo Chardonnay 1990   13 £C
Poverty Bay in provenance, but rich in fruit and hand-
somely acidic to boot.

PERUVIAN WINE – *white*

Tacama Gran Blanco 1990 14 £C
This delicious little wine is a blend of two of France's
most difficult-to-like grape varieties – ugni blanc and
chenin. Like many colonial transplants, they obviously
adore their adopted country, for the wine pulls off that
most tricky of combinations – fruity fullness with
crispness. A real find.

PORTUGUESE WINE – *red*

Arruda (Sainsbury's) 15 £B
'This wine scores so well because it has simply more
character than most wines and it costs under £2.50.' So I
wrote in the last edition of *Superplonk*. Alas, it now edges
into the B-price band but it still has a great toasted
bouquet, fruit and herbs in the mouth, and a fair old
lingering finish of woody fruit in the throat.

Bairrada 1986 13 £B
This is cheap for a wine of such aged style, but it is very
curranty and over-ripe, and needs rich food to show itself
at its best.

Dão 1985 (Sainsbury's) 12 £B

Herdade de Santa Marta 1988, Alentejo 14 £C
How does this forwards' line sound: Periquita, Alfro-
cheiro, Tinta Carvalha, Trincadeira and Moreto? They
could win the European Cup for sure – they've got style,

elegance and real attack. They are the grapes which make
up this wine and they're a fabulously fruity bunch, yet dry.

Quinta de Bacalhoa 1988   12   £C

ROMANIAN WINE – *red*

Romanian Pinot Noir (Sainsbury's)   15   £B
A better pinot noir at a quarter of the price than many a
Nuits St-Georges. Fantastic value. A smashing wine for
the price.

SPANISH WINE – *red*

La Mancha, Castillo de Alhambra 1989   15   £B
A beautifully styled fruity/dry wine. Elegantly made. Terrific value.

Navarra (Sainsbury's)   11   £B

**Viña Herminia, Luganilla, Riserva Rioja
1985**   13   £D
Either this wine is getting long in the tooth or I am. I find
the ripe quality to the vanilla edging of riojas of any age
rather unsettling. However, once harnessed to good grub
the wine comes into its own, and this one is excellent with
rice dishes and stews – especially those employing chorizo
sausage. Cooked chorizo and middle-aged rioja make a
splendid pair of cart-horses sufficient to pull the most
jaded of palates out of torpor.

SPANISH WINE – *white*

La Mancha (Sainsbury's)   13   £A
Made from the airen which covers so much of Spain that it
makes this grape variety the most extensively planted on
earth. Not surprisingly, therefore, it is a rare A-priced
wine. But this alone does not make it distinctive, for this
example is gently fruity, clean and properly put together. A
winner for heavily attended meetings of the local residents.

Moscatel de Valencia (Sainsbury's)   14   £B
A huge torrent of toffee, molasses and almonds. Terrific
value for a dessert wine of such oomph. Marvellous with
Christmas pud and cream.

Rioja 1990 (Sainsbury's)   12   £C

Valencia (Sainsbury's)   12   £A
Just over two quid a bottle can't be bad and neither is the
wine. Fresh-faced, barely apple-cheeked, and a mite puny
to finish – but at packed parties who's going to notice
anything but the pleasant, clean wine in their glasses?

USA WINE – *red*

Beaulieu, Los Carneros Reserve Pinot Noir
1988   15   £E
If you're having game, or duck or beef, or a lamb dish with
a jazzy rosemary sauce and lots of garlic, then this wine is
heaven-sent. It really is a better pinot noir for the money
than anything from the home of that grape, Burgundy. The

bouquet is an idyllic marriage of raspberries and farmyard
muck (don't be alarmed – it makes the wine smell more
authentic than many a volnay on sale in the UK) and the
taste, though perhaps betraying its Californian origins with
a faint green spiciness creeping into the full-blown fruitiness, envelops the taste-buds in a many-layered canopy.

California Cabernet Sauvignon **(Sainsbury's)**	13	£C

Jekel Vineyards Cabernet Sauvignon 1985	12	£E

La Crema Pinot Noir 1987   13   £E
This wine fails to score even higher by a whisker. Is it a
failure of the bouquet at the last gasp? A loosening of the
grip of the pinot noir taste as the wine disappears down the
gullet? The wine has class and distinction and its for-
wardness gives it some presence. Yet, in spite of these
qualities, the wine does perhaps need more age to give it
greater complexity and to heighten its character.

USA WINE – *white*

California Chardonnay (Sainsbury's)	13	£C

Sauvignon Blanc Washington State 1990 **(Sainsbury's)**	12	£C

SPARKLING WINE/CHAMPAGNE

Australian Sparkling Wine (Sainsbury's)   15   £C
Attractive bouquet. Pleasant, even complex taste. An interesting curiosity. It can be served to most people and they will say, 'Oh, this is a nice champagne.'

Cava, Spanish Sparkling Wine (Sainsbury's)   11   £C

Champagne Bonnaire Premier Cru Blanc de Blancs   14   £G
An excellent rich and dry champagne with the elegance to stand alongside the best. Good value.

Champagne Extra Dry (Sainsbury's)   15   £F
Superb at the price; biscuity, fruity and dry. Lovely champagne, so much better than the famous *marques* at more money.

Champagne Gonet, Grand Cru Blanc de Blancs   10   £G
A touch of cleanness and almost green grapes. Not wild about this on its own. A sourpuss of a champers. With a *plateau de fruits de mer*, however, it would be fine.

Crémant d'Alsace   13   £D
Some style, some class, and something for champagne-makers to think about.

Crémant de Bourgogne Rosé (Sainsbury's)   11   £D

Gratien and Meyer Cuvée Flamme Saumur   14   £D
A light, subtly fruity sparkler with a degree of justifiable pretension to finesse and dry elegance. A comfortable aperitif and can stand comparison with a decent champagne,

though it must be said it has none of a great champagne's richness.

Mercier   11   £F

Prosecco (Sainsbury's)   10   £C
It trumpets itself brassily 'a quality sparkling wine'. And a brassy beast it is.

Rosé Champagne Brut (Sainsbury's)   13   £F
Good value at this price and nicely fruity and dry.

**Sparkling Riesling 1987, Schloss
Wachenheim (Sainsbury's)**   14   £C
This is a totally agreeable aperitif wine.

Sparkling Vouvray (Sainsbury's)   14   £D
The smell of the grape, chenin blanc, should be ignored. Concentrate instead on the rounded dryness and suggestion of baked apples.

Vintage Champagne 1986 (Sainsbury's)   14   £F
Excellent value for vintage champagne, but better than the non-vintage? No way!

Spar

It was a busy *Weekend Guardian* reader who ticked me off for not including Spar in my regular survey of supermarket wines. 'How many supermarkets are open late in the evenings where I can buy a single bottle of wine when I'm rushing out to a dinner party? None. But at my local Spar I do it all the time,' I was told. Besides marvelling at this reader's hectic social life, I have to concede she has a very valid point. So I dutifully sniffed around my own local Spar and discovered not just a range of wines (which, being controlled by a proprietor who is a Spaniard, had an imbalance in favour of Rioja and Penedès) but several other interesting items as well, several of which were own-labels proudly proclaiming '1981–1991 – 8 till late – 10 years of convenient shopping'. Not, perhaps, the most engaging of messages to find haunting a wine label, or any other label for that matter, but you can't grumble about some of the prices (even though people are prepared to pay extra for 'convenient shopping').

Spar shops are owner-operated which means you may find all the wines listed here, not even one of them, or merely a selection. On the basis of my tasting of Spar wines and discussing them with the company's extremely able wine buyer I have to say that there can be few Spar shops able to procure better quality wines at better value-for-money prices. Ms Philippa Carr does all the buying herself and this single-minded approach shows itself in a consistency of type and price which is admirable. Her soave, for example, is one of the cheapest around and its presentation is as tasty as the stuff in the bottle. Her strength is Italy, in fact (her curious perfumed pear-drop valpolicella excepted), with France just behind.

Were it not for the fact that my *Guardian*-reading Spar shopper is a resident of Devon I would happily invite her to dinner – pleasantly anticipating the excellent bottle of wine in her hand. Push me and I'll admit I'd be happiest receiving a bottle of the Spar champagne, the St Hugo from Australia, or the Barbera d'Asti.

AUSTRALIAN WINE – *red*

St-Hugo Cabernet Sauvignon 1987   14   £E
Dusty drawers and oodles of brackeny blackcurrant framing the taste of tea with a subtle melon edging to the finish. A complex wine with a touch of tarry class.

FRENCH WINE – *red*

Baron Villeneuve de Cantemerle 1986   11   £E
This has a lovely bouquet but the stalky fruit in the taste lets it down – especially at the money. However, can you wait ten years? If you can, the wine will be terrific.

Cabernet Sauvignon, Vin de Pays de l'Aude 1989   12   £B

Château Plagnac 1984   13   £D
An individual style of Bordeaux with some class.

Claret 1989   10   £D
Useful size for uncritical party-goers.

Côtes du Rhône 1990 14 £A
Digestive biscuits and warm, gently toffeed fruit combine
in the mouth to make this a splendid little Rhône. An
outstanding bargain available in a conventional–sized
bottle as well as a 50-cl one – perfect for a happy solo
lunch.

Juliénas 1989 12 £D

Vin de Pays de la Cité de Carcassonne 1990 14 £B
Dry, smooth, supple – with a hint of extravagance to the
fruit. Great dinner-party plonk.

FRENCH WINE – *white*

Gewürztraminer 1989 11 £C
Grand colour. Mildly spicy. Nothing eccentric. A begin-
ner's Gewürztraminer.

Muscadet, Château des Gillières 1989 12 £C

Rosé d'Anjou 1990 13 £B
A lovely coloured rosé but with barely a bouquet worth the
name. Yet a delicious dry, biscuity fruitiness emerges from
the taste, which is very stylish. At the price, a bargain.

Sancerre, Guy Saget 1989 and 1990 10 £E
A sancerre must be more brilliant than the '89 example to
merit the name. The '90 is better with a touch of agreeably
clean fruit, but it still lacks sufficient pedigree to wear that
glorious name on its label with any pride.

GERMAN WINE – *white*

Hock   10   £B

ITALIAN WINE – *red*

Barbera d'Asti, Viticoltori deli Acquese 1989   14   £C
Excellent mouth-filling stuff. Richly endowed. Superb
Italian openness and warmth.

Chianti Classico, La Canonica 1988   13   £C
A handsome, smooth Tuscan with a firm, teeth-gripping
earthiness.

Valpolicella 1990   10   £B
If you like highly perfumed pear-drops in your mouth, this
is the wine for you.

ITALIAN WINE – *white*

Frascati Superiore, Colli de Catone 1989   10   £D

Pinot Grigio, Lageder 1989   12   £D

Soave 1990   14   £B
Firm, delicately toothed, clean with a touch of citric melon
– a classic soave. And an outstanding one for the money.
The elegance of the label gives a true picture of the wine
within.

SPANISH WINE – *red*

Rioja 13 £C

A revelation for those who think of this wine as oaky, vanilla-ey, and heavy. This is a young specimen and totally unaffected in manner, nicely balanced and unhysterical. Good value.

Valencia Red (Spar) 14 £B

One of the best-value reds in the land. An all-singing, all-dancing raspberry and blackcurrant double act. Marvellous simple stuff.

SPANISH WINE – *white*

Valencia Dry White 12 £B

Pleasant creamy fruit under the acidity. Good value.

Valencia Medium White 11 £B

Valencia Sweet White 10 £B

Grandma, over to you.

SPARKLING WINE/CHAMPAGNE

Asti Spumante 10 £D

Champagne 14 £F

A deliciously mature champagne with all the dry fruit and calm acidity you could wish for. As good as many a

marque's vintage number. Says the Spar buyer of this wine:
'It has a very loyal following and in spite of the much-
vaunted 50 per cent drop in champagne sales in the UK we
have not noticed any drop-off in our sales.' I must say I'm
not surprised.

Crémant de Loire, Gratien and Meyer   13   £D

Moscato Fizz   10   £A
This shouldn't have a score in a wine guide because technically this wine, at 4 per cent alcohol, is not wine. It is, in
truth, partially fermented grape juice. I suppose the kids
might like it, though, and old grans toothless from a
lifetime of chewing sugar.

Saumur Rosé, Gratien and Meyer   13   £D
A marvellously cheerful label introducing a marvellously
cheerful wine. It has, to be sure, that distinctive chenin
blanc grape variety bouquet (stale daisies), but the skins of
cabernet franc red wine grape variety which provide the
glorious colour give the wine body and flavour. A really
stylish champagne-substitute only snobs will ignore.

Tesco

What I like about Tesco is summed up by a remark made to me by a member of its wine-buying department while I was sampling a very inexpensive white wine from the south of France which the store had recently introduced. 'I get a real thrill finding a wine like that, simple, attractive and under £3 a bottle – especially if it helps nudge more of our customers into light, dry, modern wines and away from all those boring, characterless Liebfraumilchs and Lambruscos.' And I thought, I'm with you all the way, mate.

Tesco, you see, has a mission. And the mission has a messenger carrying a slogan. The slogan reads: TESCO GIVES YOU MOORE. Who else but Tesco could put the mockers on all its competitors by employing a comic manikin from Dagenham? Lovable cuddly Dudley sums up the new Tesco style to a T. You can bet your life the store's professional buyers worried about his satirical TV impersonation of their trade, but the marketing department stood firm, saying 'Dud is our saviour', and so the marketeers revealed a great truth to their sober-sided colleagues – modern supermarket retailing is as much about entertainment as it is about fulfilling customer's needs with the right products. Tesco's television commercials make this ideal into a reality, not just for the customers who see the films but the thousands of Tesco employees who also enjoy them. Certainly Tesco seems to say, louder than anyone else, 'We can't deny shopping can be a drag so we'll try to make it less of a chore.' The basis of this, of course, is the belief that the customer is doing *you* a favour being in *your* store and should be treated accordingly. This

117

is not in the British tradition. British retailing manners
have been in a time-warp, stalled somewhere in the late
1890s, for as long as I can remember. The modern super-
marketeers have fractured this tradition, it is true, but
Tesco is attempting to take it a stage further – to the point
where the only difference between going to the cinema and
going to the supermarket is that you queue beforehand for
one and afterwards for the other. (Indeed, when Tesco
opened their gargantuan new superstore near Aldershot
they even managed to make their customers feel not so
much like movie-goers as tourists: maps were handed out
at the doors so that people could find their way around.)

I've certainly enjoyed Tesco's supermarkets more than
I've enjoyed the majority of the films I saw in 1991. The
range of wines is considerable. The conscientious imbiber
could quaff a different Tesco wine every day for well over a
year before sampling the same bottle twice. You see, then,
the enormity of my task and what I have had to put myself
through to bring you an objective appraisal of the Tesco
range.

There are, for openers, over four dozen champagnes
(including rare items at over forty quid a bottle which this
Guide was too shy to ask to taste – besides, such wines are
only to be found at a few branches and will, I would have
thought, be guzzled only by pools winners and suchlike
who I do not expect to be in any sort of state, sensible or
otherwise, to buy this book). There are dozens of inexpensive and tasty wines, red, white and sparkling, from the
new wine-growing areas of Australia and the Americas.
And there are scores of interesting wines from the traditional wine-growing countries including, most interesting
of all, wines from the less fashionable areas of these countries – the obscurer parts of the South of France, for

example, the bandit parishes of Italy, and the ancient provincial fiefdoms of Spain where a new surge of vinous individuality, fuelled by ideas of excellence, is taking root. It is in this area that Tesco has taken initiatives like Les Domaines, a range of wines from the more mysterious wine regions of France. Suitably badged for the customers to recognize (though not boldly enough in my view), these bottles represent an encouraging trend. Nothing could be better for us wine drinkers than that the seedier wine areas get up off their knees, begin producing terrific decently-priced wines, and the po-faced, holier than thou, traditional regions, each of which charges a premium as soon as look at you, get their come-uppance.

Not surprisingly, therefore, and to carry the analogy between supermarket and cinema further, I feel a good deal more exercised at the thought of investigating this treasure-house than I do about ogling the offerings at my local flea-pit. Michelle Pfeiffer imitating Meryl Streep imitating a Russian dissident in *Russia House* is as invigorating a spectacle as watching grass grow, compared to cupping in one's hands a bottle of real honey like Tesco's Moscatel de Valencia – especially since it can be taken out of the store for a piffling £2.84.

I recommend tracking down this bottle (not difficult – most decent-sized Tescos carry it) above any cinematic adventure, with the exception of Gérard Depardieu's *Cyrano de Bergerac*. The wine is marvellous with bread and butter pudding.

ARGENTINIAN WINE – *red*

Trapiche Pinot Noir Reserve 1987   12   £B
Soft and gulpy.

ARGENTINIAN WINE – *white*

Argentinian White, Etchart   11   £B

Trapiche Chardonnay Reserve, 1990   12   £B

AUSTRALIAN WINE – *red*

Cabernet Sauvignon/Shiraz (Tesco)   15   £C
At this price, a steal. A big mouthful of dry plums and
cherried, spicy prunes. Smashing stuff with real personality .

RF Cabernet Sauvignon 1988   13   £C

Yalumba Shiraz 1987   14   £C
Purple-patched and well-balanced from nose to throat.

AUSTRALIAN WINE – *white*

Australian Chardonnay, Hardy's (Tesco)   12   £C

Australian Sauvignon, De Bortoli (Tesco)	11	£C
Australian Semillon, De Bortoli (Tesco)	12	£B

AUSTRIAN WINE – *white*

Grüner Veltliner, Winzerhaus 1990 13 £B
A happy bottle of simple wine – appealingly clean and drily fruity.

Pinot Blanc, Winzerhaus 1990 14 £B
Delicious, well-balanced wine – at home as an aperitif, with its friendly fruitiness, or, with its dashing acidity, with hors d'oeuvres and fish or salads.

CHILEAN WINE – *red*

Chilean Cabernet Sauvignon 1989 (Tesco) 14 £B
Goodness, what value for an oddly captivating gaucho with great dash and softly fruity charms!

CHILEAN WINE – *white*

Chilean Sauvignon Blanc Santa Rita 1990 13 £B
Value from first sip to last.

CHINESE WINE – *white*

Tsingtao Chardonnay 1988   12   £D
See Sainsbury's and Gateway/Somerfield for a fuller description of this curiosity. Somerfield's wine department
manager at Barking, East London, tells me the wine fairly
flies off his shelves, so perhaps Tesco will attract equally
rich customers – for the wine is expensive for the style.
Maybe you have to be barking to like it.

FRENCH WINE – *red*

Beaujolais (Tesco)   10   £C

Bois Galant, Médoc 1988   13   £D
Quite distinguished in its own way, and reasonably complex. A plateful of roast nosh best accompanies it.

Bourgueil, Domaine Hubert, La Huralaie
1989   13   £C
This red Loire wine with its raspberry and lead-pencil
flavour has long been a favourite of mine, especially when
chilled for the summer. This vintage, however, needs a
little time to soften more, but then I tasted this example in
February 1991 so by now it may be ready.

Burgundy, Henri de Bahezre NV   12   £C

Buzet, Domaine de la Croix 1988   12   £C
Hairy-bottomed maturity with this wine. Very good with
roast food and sausages.

Cabernet Sauvignon, Haute Vallée de l'Aude
(Tesco) 13 £B
Only 9p into the B price band. Excellent value for the family get-together with a roast on the table.

Château Beaulieu St-Saveur, Marmandais 13 £B
Excellent value – very dry, maturely fruity, agreeably tannic. Half a case with half a dozen friends around a candle-lit dinner table and you've got away with murder.

Château Bois Galant, Médoc 1986 13 £D
Quite distinguished in its own way, and reasonably complex. It cries out for food as Romeo cries out for Juliet.

Château d'Arsac, Cru Bourgeois, Haut-Médoc 1988 11 £D

Château de Camansac, Grand Cru Classé 1985, Haut-Médoc 12 £E

Château de Caraguilhes 1988 14 £C
The astounding truly organic wine from Corbières, an area transitionally replacing Beaujolais as the area for highly drinkable, cheap red wines. This wine needs more time to soften up a bit, but it is still a hell of a fruity mouthful.

Château des Gondats 1987 14 £C
Can a Bordeaux be taken seriously if it costs less than a fiver? Astound your friends with this one. You don't have to reveal the ridiculous price.

Château du Bluizard, Beaujolais Villages 1990 12 £C
In spite of the back label claiming that this wine's maker, Jean de St-Charle, is world-famous, his eminence has, until now, failed to penetrate the closed clam I must inhabit. His wine is OK with egg and chips.

Château les Gravières, St-Emilion 1988   14 £E
Everything you could wish for.

**Château Pigoudet, Coteaux d'Aix en Provence
1988**   14 £C
I've been prejudiced in favour of the wine from this Provence vineyard since I first went there – negotiating, I
recall, a large viper barring my way – in 1978, and found it
simple, unaggressively fruity plonk in the Côtes du Rhône
style. Now, a decade later, we have an even better wine
which has added dryness and complexity. Excellent value,
with a lovely label as a bonus.

Château St-Georges 1985, St-Emilion   10 £G
Attractive bouquet of blackcurrant and drying earth;
restrained on the fruit; green on the finish.

Château Toutigeac Bordeaux 1988   13 £C
An excellent dry berry-rich wine, typically Bordeaux in
style. Great for serious dinner parties, weighty conversa-
tions, and uncommonly rare roast beef (if there is anyone
left in the land who still indulges in any of these things).

Chinon, Baronnies Madeleine 1983   12 £D
Rare to find a Chinon of such age on a supermarket shelf.
The wine has reached its peak of maturity, however, and is
literally in its dotage. It cannot, then, get by without a stick:
in this case, food with olives and tomatoes.

Côte Rôtie 1986, Michel Bernard   12 £E

Côtes de Duras 1989   11 £B

Côtes du Frontonnais 1987   15 £B
A dry, well-structured wine with a delicious fruit presence
of blackcurrants and strawberries. At this price a terrific
bargain.

Côtes du Rhône (Tesco) 11 £B

Côtes du Rhône Villages 1989 13 £C
A much dryer style, and more fruitily mature, than basic
Côtes du Rhône. A more complex wine with a serious
expression on its face. Good with roast lamb dishes.

Domaine de Beaufort, Minervois 1988 11 £A

Domaine de Conroy, Brouilly 1988 11 £D

**Domaine des Baumelles 1989, Côtes du
Lubéron** 13 £C
This is probably Peter Mayle's house red, if he's any judge.
The author of *A Year in Provence* doesn't have to drive far to
buy it straight from the makers.

Domaine Langlois-Château, Saumur 1988 12 £D
Come on, you stubborn bottle. Let that fruit out. We know
it's in there!

Domaine les Hauts des Chambert, Cahors 13 £D
Good bit of bottle age does wonders for the right wine.

Dorgon, Vin de Pays de l'Aude 12 £A
Dry, teeth-clinging wine – very good value. Perfect for
sausages and mash (with olive oil instead of butter and lots
of black pepper).

Fitou (Tesco) 11 £B

**French Merlot, Vin de Pays de la Haute Vallée
de l'Aude** 12 £B

French Country Red (Tesco) 14 £B
A dry, fruity bargain – especially made for the parents/
teachers get-together with huge bowls of garlicky
ratatouille.

Gevrey-Chambertin, Marchand 1987   10   £F

**Hautes Côtes de Nuits, Caves des Hautes
Côtes 1988**   12   £D

**Hautes Côtes de Beaune, Les Caves des
Hautes Côtes 1987**   14   £D
A true gamy pinot noir from Burgundy at an acceptable
price. Balanced and fruity in a smashing guzzle-worthy
way. Great value for an expensive style – a wine to
restore the area's reputation when so much burgundy is
over-produced, over-filtered, over-pasteurized, over-
chaptalized (i.e. too much sugar), over-priced and, sadly,
over here.

Les Terres Fines Cépage 1989, Syrah   10   £B

Médoc (Tesco)   11   £C

Morgon, Arthur Barolet 1988   12   £D

Red Burgundy (Tesco)   11   £C

**Savigny les Beaune, Hospices de Beaune
1986**   12   £F

St-Emilion (Tesco)   12   £C

Vin de Pays des Bouches du Rhône (Tesco)   13   £B
The usual sort of thing; fruity, floral smell, good body.
Very good value. Very amiable with fish dishes (which is
hardly surprising as there's a touch of seaweed on the
finish).

**Vin de Pays des Coteaux de la Cité de
Carcassonne 1989, Sica Foncalieu**   12   £A
Very dry. Nice touch of fruit, though.

Vin de Pays des Côtes de Gascogne Yvon Mau	11	£A
Vin de Pays des Collines Rhodaniennes 1987, Syrah	13	£B

FRENCH WINE – *white*

Alsace Gewürztraminer 1988 (Tesco)	10	£C
Alsace Pinot Blanc, Caves de l'Enfer (Tesco)	12	£B
Alsace Riesling, Caves de l'Enfer (Tesco)	11	£C
Beaujolais Blanc 1989	12	£C
Burgundy, Caves des Hautes Côtes	13	£D

A respectable effort – oaky and fruity.

Cabernet de Saumur 1989, Caves des Vignerons de Saumur	14	£B

The cabernet franc grape makes a very interesting rosé, and this particular example also has a lovely colour and a good firm structure. Dry, yet with sufficient fruit to survive chilling. Good value at under £3.

Cépage Terret, Vin de Pays de l'Hérault, Delta Domaines 1990	13	£B

Good balance, good price, good by itself.

Chablis 1989 (Tesco)	12	£D
Château de Carles, Sauternes 1989	12	£F

Yes, it's a lot of dosh but it's a lot of posh – a fine full sauternes with all the honey, molasses (burnt) and creamy

fruit you could wish for. But is it four times better than
Tesco's Moscatel de Valencia? Only if a real aficionado is
coming to dinner and you must seduce him or her at all costs.

Château les Girotins, Sauternes 1989 (half)   13   £D
Luscious pudding wine, in a handy helping (exclusive to
Tesco) with all the honeyed effect you could wish for.
Delightful.

Château Magneau, Graves 1989   14   £E
A gorgeous smoky, woody, raspberry-ringed clean wine
which even at this price makes you rejoice and throw all your
worries out the window. A lovely mouthful.

Château Vert Bois 1990   13   £C
A refreshing little wine made, appropriately, by a man called
tea.

**Châteauneuf-du-Pape, Les Arnevels, Quiot
1990   14   £D**
White Châteauneuf-du-Pape is not to everyone's taste with
its curious soft, slightly creamy, very dry style (the Food
Editor of *Weekend Guardian*, a man of immense liberality of
palate, can't stand the stuff), but this example begs to be
tried. It is a lovely wine, dry yet cheekily fruity, with a
gorgeous underlying acidity.

**Domaine de Collin Rozier Chardonnay, Vin
de Pays d'Oc 1989   13   £D**

**Domaine de Jalousie, Late Harvest 1989,
Grassa   12   £C**
A very engaging pre-prandial tipple. The touch of treacle on
the fruit (while, paradoxically, clean) is quite pleasant. But
as a dessert wine, forget it.

Domaine de la Jalousie, Cuvée Bois 1989 13 £C
Happy integration of wood and fruit. And no overdosing of
the latter, either. A charming little wine.

**Domaine St-Alain de Pays des Côtes du
Tarn** 11 £B

Entre-Deux-Mers (Tesco) 12 £B
Having dinner with this wine-maker's family, I was
proudly shown the fruits of the senior member's recent
gallstone operation (see page 84); this wine contains no
such surprises nor is it so aromatic, but if you want simple
Bordeaux blanc, this is it.

**Escoubes, Vin de Pays des Côtes de Gascogne
1990 (Tesco)** 13 £B
February tasting: A pleasant, melony wine at a good price
from the pioneer of drinkable white Gascon hooch, Monsieur Grassa (not the most felicitous of names for a wine-
grower, it sits better on a groundsman or a Mafia stool
pigeon, but this does not mar the pleasure of drinking the
stuff).

April tasting: A cleaner vintage, the 1990, than the previous ones. Less fruit, more elegant acidity – good wine at
a brilliant price.

French Country White (Tesco) 13 £C
A Côtes de Gascogne in origin but with none of the
booming fruit – instead, the pineapples and peaches and
lemons combine most happily to make a happy little wine.
Excellent value.

Graves, Yvon Mau (Tesco) 11 £C

**Les Terres Fines, Cépage Muscat 1987, Delta
Domaines**   12   £C
Pleasant summer aperitif, but a mite sharpish on the finish.

Les Terres Fines, Muscat Sec 1990   12   £C
A summer garden aperitif rather than a dessert wine. I
suppose you could drink it in the house with the central
heating at full blast.

Mâcon Blanc Villages 1989 (Tesco)   13   £C
Second-best in tasting of white burgundies. Clean smell
and finish. Good with seafood risotto and similar complex
fish dishes.

**Menetou-Salon, Domaine de la Montaloise
1988**   12   £C

Monbazillac (Tesco)   12   £C

**Muscadet Sur Lie, Domaine de la Huperie
1989**   12   £C

Muscat Cuvée Jose Sala   15   £B
There are few such honey-toffeed dessert wines around at
this price. Not as deep and as rich as a pricier Beaumes de
Venise or first-growth sauternes, but what do you expect
for such a small amount?

Pouilly Blanc Fumé, Les Berthiers 1989   10   £E

Premières Côtes de Bordeaux (Tesco)   11   £B

Sancerre, Alphonse Mellot 1989   10   £E

Sauvignon Blanc (Tesco)   13   £B
Excellent value – dry, clean and melony fruit.

St-Romain Blanc, Arthur Barolet 1987   11   £D

| Vin de Pays de la Dordogne, Sigoules | 12 | £B |

| Vin de Pays des Coteaux des Baronnies, Chardonnay 1990 | 11 | £B |

The des's don't add up to a des. res. as far as the chardon-nay is concerned. If it's at home, it doesn't answer the door. Still, you can't grumble with the freshness of the wine or the price.

| Vouvray, Chevalier de Moncontour Brut 1987 | 13 | £D |

| White Burgundy, Les Caves des Hautes Côtes 1987 | 13 | £C |

This isn't a bad bash at producing a decent white bur-gundy, but only as long as the price stays below a fiver. Over that, and its clean yet fruity style has severe competi-tion. Made by a co-op in Beaune which combines modern vinification methods whilst retaining traditions like ageing in oak casks.

GERMAN WINE – *white*

| Baden Dry | 13 | £B |

You'd never credit this dry yet fruity wine with being a Kraut: yet a very pleasant blonde specimen, this.

| Bereich Johannisberg Riesling, Krayer 1989 | 11 | £B |

| Bernkasteler Kurfurstlay Riesling 1989 (Tesco) | 10 | £B |

**Brauneberger Kurfurstlay Riesling Kabinett
1990, Paulinshof**   12   £C
Delicious aperitif: fragrant, light and not at all sweet. (This
wine comes in two versions, of which this is the medium
dry and costs 10p less. The other also scores 12, but I
slightly prefer the above.)

Hock (Tesco)   11   £A

**Johannisberger Klaus, Riesling, Schloss
Schönborn 1988**   11   £C

**Johannisberger Klaus, Riesling, Schloss
Schönborn 1989**   11   £C

**Kreuznacher Narrenkappe, Riesling Auslese,
Anheuser 1976**   14   £E
Imagine cream, honey and nuts liquidized and left for
yonks to blend brilliantly. This wine is all that in a glass.
Lovely with pud, with ice-cream even (legendarily, an
impossible partner for wine), or with fresh fruit.

Morio Muskat   12   £B
Good grapey aperitif.

Mosel Medium Dry Riesling (Tesco)   11   £B

Niersteiner Gutes Domtal   12   £A

**Niersteiner Pettenthal, Riesling Spätlese,
Balbach 1985**   11   £D

**Piesporter Treppchen, Riesling Kabinett
1990**   12   £C
Pre-prandial Piesporter.

Rauenthaler Rothenberg, Riesling 1988   11   £C

Rheinpfalz Dry Riesling 12 £B
Drunk chilled, in the garden, as a taste-bud tickler, this wine is fine. Or try it with sparkling mineral water as a spritzer.

Rheinpfalz Medium Dry Silvaner 10 £B

Ruppertsberger Hoheberg, Riesling 1987 13 £C
This is a halbtrocken wine, which means it is half-dry. This does not mean, though, that the other half is sweet. On the contrary, this wine has the muscular elegance to be most acceptable with a Sunday lunch of roast pork with apple sauce.

Saar Tafelwein (Tesco) 13 £A
At under £2.50 this is an agreeable aperitif with its melony aroma and aftertaste, and with its pleasant medium-bodied style good with food for those who dislike bone-dry whites.

St-Johanner Abtei Kabinett (Tesco) 11 £B

St-Johanner Abtei Spätlese (Tesco) 12 £B
Nice with a fresh, crisp apple and a chunk of cheese.

Steinweiler Kloster Liebfrauenberg Auslese (Tesco) 12 £C

Steinweiler Kloster Liebfrauenberg Kabinett (Tesco) 10 £B

Steinweiler Kloster Liebfrauenberg Spätlese (Tesco) 11 £C

Stettener Stein, Franken 11 £C
Vigorous, appley, dry wine of interest to oyster-lovers. The bottle makes a handsome lampshade when empty (or even full if you like to live dangerously).

Trittenheimer Altarchen, Riesling 1988 12 £D

HUNGARIAN WINE – *red*

Merlot, Villany 1989 (Tesco)   14   £A
Very good value. Excellent; soft, drinkable stuff.

HUNGARIAN WINE – *white*

Hungarian Chardonnay (Tesco)   10   £B

ITALIAN WINE – *red*

Barbaresco (Tesco) 1983   14   £D
An excellent mature wine with personality and style. Perfect with rich Italian main-course dishes.

Barolo, Giacosa Fratelli 1984   13   £D
That sour liquorice taste just explodes under food like pasta with burnt bacon and garlic.

Barolo Riserva Chiarlo 1982   13   £F
A lot of money for a lot of wine. But a cool-headed barolo for all that. None of those sweaty hairy armpits swimming with liquorice as with many a barolo – just pleasant fruit and firmly herbal undertones.

Briccoviole, Sebaste 1987   13   £E
Stylish fruitwise and interestingly creamy. Might be best to keep it for a few years before drinking it. Don't let the Vino da Tavola designation put you off. This wine, made from a

highly individual blend of nebbiolo and barbera grape
varieties, offends Italian wine laws. It can't call itself barolo
for a start, even though it is made there.

Cabernet Sauvignon Ca Donini 1989   13   £C
No sour grapes with this Italian copy of a French
masterpiece; just lots of fruit, masses of quaffability, and
tons of value.

Chianti Classico (Tesco) 1988   14   £B
Soft in a hairy-chested sort of way – husky-voiced and
floral. But not quite as integrated as the cheaper chianti
below and not, as a result, so immediately likeable.

Chianti Rufina, Grati 1989   14   £B
Delicious dry stuff – an exceptional chianti for the money.
Has all the gruff-mannered elegance of the type and it
seems to reek of Tuscan terracotta fruitiness.

Chianti (Tesco) 1989   16   £B
Easily one of the best chiantis around for the brilliant value
for money it represents. An immediately attractive and very
drinkable wine with lots of fruit and Tuscan earthiness. It
is around 60p cheaper than the supposed superior Classico
above and it ought to be less good, but it isn't.

Franciacorta II Mosnel 1988   14   £C
Cabernet/merlot/nebbiolo/barolo – what an astounding
twinning of Pomerol and Milan through their neighbour-
hood grape varieties. This has a heavenly aroma (roses)
and a taste of sun-filled blackcurrants with creamy figs.
Lovely stuff.

Merlot del Piave (Tesco)   12   £B

Monte Firidolfi, Chianti Classico 1987   14   £C
Woody, husky, fruity.

Montepulciano d'Abruzzo, Bianchi 1989   13   £C
A chewy wine of great merit with pastas and the like.

Montepulciano d'Abruzzo, Villa Paola 1987   13   £C
Gorgeous, gooey stuff for two passionate, but as yet
unconnected, would-be lovers to become mellow about
whilst consuming spaghetti with bacon or some-such.

**Orfeno Vino da Tavola Rosso dell'Uccellina
1989   14   £C**
Made from sangiovese and ciltegiolo grapes in the Parco
Naturale Della Maremma Park in Tuscany, this wine is
organically grown and this may or may not (I am not
technically capable of judging) account for the wine's
undoubted fresh earthy appeal. The addition of the
uncommon ciltegiolo grape variety adds a softness to the
fiery sangiovese (which makes chianti) and the result is a
delightfully unassuming yet rich wine of rustic fruitiness
which to me at least tastes like an old-fashioned chianti
ought to taste anyway.

Recioto della Valpolicella 1985   14   £D
This is made from semi-dried grapes and it shows in a
distinguished curranty wine which is all-embracingly fruity
yet dry. Marvellous with stews and roasts which feature
dried fruits, but especially toothsome with rich cheeses
(blue and goat's).

Rosso Rubino 1986   14   £B
Nothing but charm. Full, fruity and dry, quintessentially
Italian in its fully integrated no-nonsense approachability.
Remarkable value for money for a wine of such stylish
maturity.

Sicilian Red (Tesco)   14   £B
A fruity, spirited little thing with a finish recalling the smell

of Ferrari tyres rising off the autostrada. Nice, warm, rubbery mouthful of fruit. A smashing wine to enjoy with lots of friends and masses of pasta dripping with garlic.

Valle del Sole Barbera, Gallo d'Oro 1986   12   £E

Villa di Monte, Chianti Rufina 1986   13   £C

Villa di Monte, Chianti Rufina Reserva 1979   11   £D
Chianti this mature does not grow on trees and there is barely a year of life left in this particular example. It seems to have lost the exuberance and freshness of youth and wilted to a rather unremarkable and tired old age. Nevertheless it would partner spaghetti carbonara without disgracing itself.

ITALIAN WINE – *white*

Chardonnay, Alto Adige, E. Von Keller 1990   15   £C
Perfect wine, perfectly priced. Lovely graceful entrance of the fruit hand-in-hand with the acidity, like two angels. A master-class in simple chardonnay-making at a reasonable sum.

Chardonnay del Veneto (Tesco)   14   £B
A perfect little chardonnay of pleasant fruitiness and charming acidic balance. Outstanding value for money at under £3.

Cicogna Pinot Bianco, Colli Berici 1988   13   £D
Good value.

Colli Albani, Cantina Sociale 1990 (Tesco)   12   £B
Interesting: soft and fruity yet with a curious nutty tang.

Frascati (Tesco)   13   £B

Naragus di Cagliari, Dolianova 1989   14   £B
I'm happy to drink this wine any time (even with breakfast).
Excellent bitter/fruity dry wine. Good as an aperitif or with
shellfish dishes.

Orvieto Classico Abboccato 1989 (Tesco)   12   £B

Orvieto Classico Secco Vaselli DOC 1990   12   £C

**Pinot Grigio del Veneto, Vino da Tavola 1989
(Tesco)**   13   £C

Pinot Grigio, Tiefenbrunner 1989   12   £C
A touch more acidity than fruitiness gives this wine the
backbone to handle all kinds of fish.

Sicilian White (Tesco)   14   £B
A bargain of a drinkable wine for slurping in vast quantities
by itself or with pasta and seafood dishes.

Soave Classico (Tesco)   12   £B

Terre di Ginestra 1990   13   £C
Grown in bandit country (i.e. in Sicily) from a single
honest grape variety, the cataratto. Under a toothy, fruity
cloak it hides a steely touch.

**Terre Toscano, Cantina del Vini Tipici 1990
(Tesco)**   13   £B
Nice prickle with this one.

**Toscano, Bianco Vergine Val di Chiana DOC
1990**   12   £B

**Verdicchio dei Castelli di Jesi Classico 1990
(Tesco)** 13 £C
Imagine having to ask for this wine. At Tesco you merely
have to take it off the shelf. And once opened, ignore the
wet-wool bouquet and concentrate on the lovely fruit and
faint bitter echo of almonds.

MEXICAN WINE – *red*

L.A. Cetto Mexican Cabernet Sauvignon 13 £C
How well would this wine shift if it said Baja California
instead of Mexico on the label, as legitimately it could? A
creamy, elegant wine of substance and class and high value.

NEW ZEALAND WINE – *white*

Stoneleigh Chardonnay 1989 13 £D

PORTUGUESE WINE – *red*

Bairrada 1987 (Tesco) 13 £B

Dão 1985 (Tesco) 13 £B
Velvety fruit, worth investing in at this price.

Douro 1982 (Tesco) 14 £B
Nice price for a mature, fruity wine of restrained elegance.

Not showy or over-woody – made for that evening meal with pasta or a complex salad with sun-dried tomatoes and olives.

Garrafeira PT81 Fonseca 1981   15   £D
February tasting note: 14 points. On the way to greatness. Big cigars and chocolate and dried fruit. Terrific with rich foods.

April tasting note: 15 points. How possible? Ten years old and under a fiver? Buy as much as you can afford of this brilliant husky, raspberry-and-blackberry yet very mature wine. Elegance and peasant burliness wrestling in a very drinkable way.

Quinta da Cardiga Ribatejo   11   £A

PORTUGUESE WINE – *white*

Bairrada, Sogrape 1990   13   £B
Perfectly pitched price, perfectly pitched acidity.

Casa Portuguesa White   11   £B

SPANISH WINE – *red*

Don Darias, Vino de Mesa, Alto Ebro   10   £A

Gran Don Darias   13   £B
February tasting notes: the combination of oak and fruit is petting heavily but not yet ready to have a serious relationship and settle down. Kept for a little while, though, a

dream marriage might emerge from the bottle.

May tasting notes: that Methuselah on the label is beginning to appear an appropriate symbol: the wine smells ancient but the fruit on the tongue is still youthful. If not yet wed, the fruit and oak are now properly engaged. Buy the wine for the bravura of the whole production.

November: hallelujah! Throw the confetti!

Rioja (Tesco) 13 £C
Delicious, controlled rioja in a lighter vein than the hot-blooded, vanilla-flavoured variety we've learned to loathe. Pretty wine.

Rioja Reserva 1983 (Tesco) 13 £D
In spite of a slight overkill of vanilla from the oak ageing, a firm, fruity specimen. It yells out for food to be consumed with it.

Señorio de Guanianeja, Cabernet Sauvignon, Gran Riserva 1983 12 £D
Quercus alba makes this quirky stuff. *Quercus alba* is American oak and this wine is mollycoddled by it for three long years before bottling. The result, always interesting, is the smell of sherry vanilla and the taste of blackcurrant sorbet. Intriguing.

SPANISH WINE – *white*

Don Darias White, Vino da Mesa 12 £A

Moscatel de Valencia (Tesco) 15 £B
If there is such a thing as a peasant dessert wine, this is it.

So rich it would overpower dessert grapes, but not bread-and-butter pud. (Try this wine with that very British afters just once and, I promise, you'll kill to get seconds.)

Rioja, Bodegas Abalos	10	£C
Rioja (Tesco)	10	£C
Viña Amalia, Vinicola del Sur	12	£B
Viña del Castillo Blanco	12	£B

The airen grape variety makes this wine. Have you ever heard of it? Of course not. Most people outside Spain stay in happy ignorance of its existence, yet there is more airen planted (all in Spain) than any other grape on earth. Tasting this wine, one is given a glimpse of the reason for this strict parochialism; for though this example has a very modern, clean taste there is barely any discernible fruit whatsoever. Worth its 12 points, though, at its price, as an agreeable partner to shellfish.

Vinaodiel, Condada Huelva, 1990	11	£B

USA WINE – *red*

Bethel Heights Pinot Noir 1987	12	£E

Too jammy and sweet for dyed-in-the-wool pinot noir lovers, but, that said, try this wine with gamy, festive dishes with fruity stuffings, and it will perform well.

Californian Red (Tesco)	13	£B

An interesting blend of cabernet sauvignon and barbera grape varieties. (Oh, the marvellous freedom given New World wine-makers to experiment when the Bordelais and the Piedmontese would shudder at the thought of their grape varieties becoming wed in this way!) And how do the Yanks do it for so few francs?

Fetzer Californian Cabernet Sauvignon 1985 13 £C
A very fruity, oaky wine of determined character with a working-class background rather than an upper-middle, which would successfully enhance pizzas and suchlike.

Jack London Cabernet Sauvignon 1986 11 £F
The only wine I know of which provides an extract from a novel (see back label).

ZD Pinot Noir Napa Valley 1986 11 £F

USA WINE – *white*

Fetzer Valley Oaks Fumé 1987 13 £D

The Hogue Cellars Chardonnay Reserve 14 £E
Lovely style. Quite distinguished and elegant. Not at all tinned, over-fruity or coarse.

SPARKLING WINE/CHAMPAGNE

Asti Spumante (Tesco) 10 £C

Ayala Champagne Brut NV 14 £G
A delightful aperitif champagne.

Blancs de Blancs Champagne (Tesco) 12 £A

Cava (Tesco)   11 £C

Champagne (Tesco)   13 £F
Very good value. Even at this moderately respectable score
it is better than most big *marques* – dry, with a good acid
balance.

Chardonnay Spumante   11 £C

**Crémant de Loire Rosé, Cave des Vignerons de
Saumur**   12 £D

Del Colle Rosso Spumante   11 £B

**Deutz, Marlborough Cuvé 1988, New
Zealand**   11 £F
Just like Deutz champagne from the well-known Rheims
company. Uncanny resemblance, but a lot of money for a
copy of the real thing. Having said that, the grape varieties
are the same and the vinification and ageing process is
precisely that of champagne. And Deutz happily license
Montana in New Zealand to make it. Unhappily, such
wine, unvictimized by champagne grape-growers' prices
and not subject to any restrictive practices, should be
£6.50, not well over a tenner – otherwise why bother to
trudge all the way to the world's biggest sheep farm to
produce it?

Grand Duchess Brut Sparkling Wine, Russia 10 £C
Almost no flavour, elegance or class whatsoever. A prole
brew which perestroika is unlikely to affect. Made near
Odessa, the Blackpool of Russia – specially, I imagine, for
all those Siberian miners on their annual hols.

Moscato d'Asti Gallo d'Oro   13 £C
A great peachy, pear-like sparkling wine which is marvellous with pud.

Niersteiner Gutes Domtal (Tesco) 11 £D

Soave Classico Spumante DOC 13 £D
Made to sip with almonds, a glass of this before dinner is a
brilliant idea. (And the brain-dead among your guests will
say, 'I like this champagne.')

**Vintage Champagne Premier Cru 1983
(Tesco)** 11 £G

Waitrose

Waitrose has fewer own-labels than any other supermarket. Its wine-buying department puts its individual stamp on the bottles the store sells in less superficially obvious ways. It's been the only store, for example, to offer wines from South Africa for me to taste, it was the first to ask me to taste Indian champagne, and it has been the only store to be so stung by one of my harsher crits that it sent me fresh samples along with the sincere plea that I re-evaluate the wine (which was a civilized way of saying I didn't know what I was talking about).

Waitrose scorns fancy labels and designer packaging. Breeze into one of its stores and the wine department stands there like a kindly, benevolent, uncommunicative ancient uncle – just hanging around waiting for some kind soul to take pity on it, ask how it feels today, and maybe take a bottle or two off the shelves. There's less coercion, either from strategically placed special offers or enticingly conjured designer labels, than from any of its competitors.

'We do not care to advertise our presence on our customers' dinner tables,' a wine buyer told me. 'Apart from the odd own-label bottle, we keep to the wine-makers' own labels.' Therefore, look not for badges of in-store approval on Waitrose bottles; there is no equivalent of Sainsbury's Vintage Selection or M & S Connoisseur's Collection or Tesco's Les Domaines.

Yet does any other supermarket wine-buying department buy more skilfully? Buy more adventurously? Is any other supermarket more dextrous at mixing the inexpensive bargain with the high-priced yet genuinely high-falutin' bottle? It is arguable. At Waitrose, shelf by shelf if not exactly cheek by jowl, you can shell out all of £20 on a Puligny Montra-chet or just £2.85 on a Blanc de Mer – and in either case you are rewarded with a special white wine.

They also like the pinot noir grape variety at Waitrose, you'll discover – in all its various forms and appellations from around the globe. By all means get your nose into a glass of wine-maker Boillot's volnay (£12.50) if you like your pinot noir in classic Burgundian form, but don't turn it up at the thought of the unusual pinot noir from Alsace, Cuvée à l'Ancienne (£6.55), or the example from Cali-fornia called Barrow Green (£7.95). Pinot noir is a bitch to grow and a tricky customer to mature congenially, but Waitrose has bottles which make light of these problems.

The store also has very interesting inexpensive white wines (in addition to the marvellous Blanc de Mer men-tioned above). Two of the most interesting, with luxury flavours deliciously balanced by plebeian price tags, are Jacquère 1989 (£4.15) and Domaine de Bellevue 1989 (£4.25). Jacquère is a little-known grape which thrives near the Swiss border, so has an unfashionable image, and Domaine de Bellevue is a St-Pourcain which hardly any-one has heard of or cares about though it was a renowned medieval name in France.

You can put both these wines on any dinner table in the land, except the most severely barbaric, and draw from your guests, or whoever it is you wish to seduce, only the most complimentary of comments along the lines of 'Goodness, isn't this wine delicious.' This is followed by a pause and then, 'Where on earth did you find it?' And you, wily Waitrose shopper that you are, can respond with 'Oh, I just happen to know a wine merchant who goes in for delicious curiosities.'

You will, of course, be speaking the truth.

ARGENTINIAN WINE – *red*

Trapiche 1988   13   £B
Very good-value, stylish wine.

AUSTRALIAN WINE – *red*

**Hardy's Premium Classic
Dry Red 1988**   13 (going on 15?)   £B
Cabernet sauvignon and shiraz double-act at an astonish-
ing price. Laying it down for a year will bring it out even
more and make it a higher-scoring wine of considerable
class and distinction. That dizzily rich fruitiness is more
suggested at than as hugely forward as it could be.

Leasingham Domaine Shiraz 1989   13   £C
They must use the scrapings from a kangaroo's pouch to
give this wine its glorious spicy animal-leathery character.
Smashing stuff for barbecued foods.

AUSTRALIAN WINE – *white*

Hardy's Early Bird 1990   14   £C
No wonder the laughing kokaburra on the label is so called
– it is chuckling at this cheeky little blend of sherbet
lemon/charentais melon ice-cream and water-ice. An
interesting, refreshing wine.

Houghton Gold Reserve, Chardonnay 1988	12	£C
Houghton Gold Reserve, Verdelho 1988	11	£D
Michelton, Marsanne 1988	11	£D

Mitchelton Fumé Blanc 1989, Victoria   11   £D
A wine which pushes the boat out for you label-wise.

AUSTRIAN WINE – *white*

Grüner Veltliner 1989   13   £C
An odd wine made from the eponymous grüner veltliner
grape variety which is only grown, as far as I know, in
Austria. It has a degree of engaging fruitiness and is clean
and respectable with it, but a curious bright zesty quality
lurks within it, rather like a sober civil servant who secretes
floral underpants beneath his pinstripes. Well worth its
rating, though, as long as it doesn't go over the four quid
mark.

BULGARIAN WINE – *red*

Mavrud 1983, Assenovgrad   13   £B
A merlot with rich overtones and a toasted dryness helping
the fruit along.

Merlot/Gamza   13   £A

CHILEAN WINE – *red*

Concha y Toro, Cabernet Sauvignon 1986   14   £C
I said of the '85 vintage of this wine that it was one to put to
the decanter test; shrouded in lead crystal twinkling under
candlelight, it will cozen many folk into thinking it an
arty-farty bordeaux of an ancient château. The '86 is like-
minded but not as devious; though it rates as highly for the
subtle touches of chocolate and toffee giving it a mellow
fruitiness of considerable charm.

ENGLISH WINE – *white*

Carr Taylor Reichensteiner 1989   12   £C

FRENCH WINE – *red*

Bourgogne Hautes-Côtes de Beaune 1988   13   £D

Buzet 1988   14   £B
A carefully made wine from an area which used legitimately to call itself part of Bordeaux. It's more open and
approachable than a claret, however, though no less elegant. It has firm fruit and a woody edge. And its style has
some finesse.

Cabardes VDQS 1988   14   £B
Soft and supple, with a gritty edge. Very attractive.

Château Bourdac 1988   11   £D

Château Cayrou Monpezat 1986, Cahors   13   £C

Château d'Agassac 1986, Ludon
Haut-Médoc   13   £E
Very dark colour. Nice soft fruity nose. Pleasant, well-
balanced wine, very easy to drink.

Château de Lucat 1986, Premières Côtes de
Bordeaux   13   £C
Excellent little claret. Good with roast lamb and more
formal dishes.

Château de Nages 1990, Costières de Nimes   13   £B
A warm, fruity soup of a wine which, though indistinct in
aroma, is firm and full in the taste department.

Château de Prade 1988   11   £C

Château Grand-Puy-Lacoste 1987   12   £F
A famous old name best kept in a dark place for a decade
before opening. Needs another five years to show itself off at
its lip-smackin' best.

Château La Fleur-Pipeau 1987, St-Emilion
Grand Cru   14   £D
Fruity and well made – a true claret.

Château Marseau 1989, Côtes du Marmandais
VDQS   10   £B
The previous vintage of this wine scored 14. It may be that
the '89 needs time to blossom. If so, you only have to venture
£2.95 to find out.

Château Plantey 1987, Pauillac   14   £D
I love that touch of bitterness with the fruit. An excellent wine.

Claret, Patrice Calvet 1986, Bordeaux   12   £C

Côtes de Duras 1988, Seigneuret   13   £B
A bargain wine for a roast lunch.

Côtes du Rhône 1989 (Waitrose)   14   £B

Crozes-Hermitage 1987/88, Cave des Clairmonts   10   £C

Dame Adelaide 1988   13   £C
Sounds like an Aussie drag queen, but is, in fact, a sober-sided citizen with quite an aristocratic fruity dryness to it.

Domaine de Beauséjour 1989   11   £B

Domaine de la Solitude, Châteauneuf-du-Pape 1988, Lancon   12   £D

Domaine de St-Macaire, Vin de Pays de l'Hérault   11   £A
Made by Baron de Rascas who, nominally at least, deserves encouragement. This wine needs more fruit to score higher than it does.

Domaine du Petit Clocher 1989, Anjou Rouge   12   £B

Gamay Haut-Poitou 1990   12   £B

Gevrey-Chambertin Premier Cru Les Cazatiers 1986   13   £G
A lot of smackers for a wine a lot of people will cover with kisses.

Good Ordinary Claret Bordeaux (Waitrose)   13   £B

Hautes Côtes de Beaune 1988, Caves des Hautes Côtes   13   £C

| Les Forts de Latour 1984, Pauillac | 13 | £G |

| Marsannay 1987, Raisin Social | 13 | £E |

Nuits-St-Georges 1988, Caves des Hautes Côtes   10   £F
Scandalous price for a wine of no great shakes.

Pinot Noir d'Alsace, Cuvée Ancienne 1988   15   £D
One of the glories of Alsatian viticulture, this utterly beguiling wine (rich and gamy, yet fresh and satiny) is great well chilled with almost everything from fish to pork sausages. It is absolutely one of my favourite wines at Waitrose – OK, in the whole wide world of wine.

Sarget de Gruaud Larose 1984, St-Julien   13   £E
A pungent, meaty bordeaux. Second wine of an efficient vineyard which is always good but always a mite dull.

Savigny-les-Beaune 1988, Faiveley   No rating   £E
I said of the previous vintage of this wine (in giving it all of 17 points) that the pinot noir has never been better put together for under a tenner in my experience. At the time of going to press I have yet to taste the 1988 but I have sufficient faith in its maker to believe that it would be nothing less than interesting – hence I include it here as worthy of your attention, although I cannot rate it.

| Special Reserve Claret (Waitrose) | 12 | £C |

| Special Reserve Claret 1986, Bordeaux | 12 | £C |

St-Amour 1989, Les Poulets (half)   13   £C
A useful half-bottle. The wine is extremely rich for a young beaujolais, even for a cru like St-Amour which habitually turns in a meaty wine. Useful size for timid drinkers, but a pricey bottle of beaujolais.

St-Chinian	11	£A

St-Joseph 1988, Cave de St-Désirat 16 £D
A wine bearing the name of the patron saint of cuckolds
has to be worth investigating, and this bottle certainly is. It
is a red wine so tasty and all-enveloping that given the
choice between a wife and a bottle many a man, cuckold or
not, might well pick the bottle. It is extremely forward, with
a marvellous rich, jammy mélange of berried fruits at the
dry end of the spectrum.

Vieux Château Gaubert 1988 14 £D
A seriously made, woody and fruity claret. More musky
than elegance would permit, but a nice blackcurranty,
mature style.

FRENCH WINE – *white*

Alsace Gewürztraminer 1989	12	£C
Beaujolais Blanc 1989, Bully	13	£C

Blanc de Mer 16 £B
I groaned when I saw this wine. That name! That label!
The worst kind of abomination which the worst type of
Côte d'Azur seafront café, overcharging the simple-
minded tourist like mad, has fronting its house wine. The
back label makes one suspicious, too, with its description
of the wine as 'dry, fresh and crisp with an amazing depth
and intensity of fruit flavour'. And, lastly, who is this Pierre
Guéry named on the label? And where on earth is La
Chapelle-Huelin where his vineyard is? But what do you
know? (Or, rather, what do *I* know?) The wine is bloody

marvellous stuff and absolutely glorious with all kinds of
fish and tastes exactly like the back label says it does.
Monsieur Guéry, you are a cunning genius – if you'd put
muscadet on the label, as you could have done, I suspect,
and charged us two-and-a-half times the price, we'd all
pass by the other side of the street with our noses in the air.
As it is, Waitrose, no less cunning than M. Guéry, are
handing us one of the wine bargains of the year.

Bordeaux 1988 Patrice Calvet   13   £C
A delicious, slightly baked aroma with the oak-aged fruit
providing a goodly rounded white with a clean finish.

Bordeaux Sauvignon Sec 1990   13   £B

Bourgogne Aligoté 1990, Brocard   13   £C
Not a bad wine – reminiscent of a sauvignon at its steely/
fruity best.

Bourgogne Blanc 1988, Cave de Buxy   11   £C

Cabernet Rosé Haut-Poitou VDQS 1989   13   £B
A very good rosé for the money. Summer barbecue wine,
really.

Chablis 1989, Alain Couperot (half)   13   £C
What a useful size. And what a pleasant wine.

Chablis 1989, Gaec des Réugnis   16   £D
No, not cheap. But it is an utterly captivating chablis. It has
a slightly smoky mix of butter and fruit, undercut by a
freshness and vigour which is typical of the style. Worth
every penny. Treat it as a special white burgundy for rich
fish dishes, if it'll make you feel better.

Chardonnay Haut-Poitou 1989   13   £C

Chardonnay, Vin de Pays du Jardin de la France   11   £C

Château Bastor-Lamontagne 1988, Sauternes (half)   13   £C
Useful half-bottle of dessert wine for small dinner parties: rich, honeyed and ripe on the nose.

Château Darzac 1990   13   £C
A delicious balance of cleanness and fruitiness. Shellfish will die for it.

Château de Rochemorin 1989, Pessac-Leognan   14   £D
A serious-looking bottle containing a seriously good wine. Cunningly, I offered a glass, anonymously, to a rival supermarket wine buyer (a man with an awesome reputation for knowing his onions) to taste and he said 'Magic'.

Château Jolys, Jurançon Moelleux 1988   12   £E
A pity this interesting wine is this price. It's hopelessly poor value compared with some of the cheaper sauternes, not to mention some of the treacly efforts from Spain. Best kept for donkey's years before opening, during which time it might blossom into something wonderful. At the moment the fruit is restrained, and the acidity over-embracing and the total effect is unbalanced – even a fruit like a pineapple will simply overwhelm the wine.

Château Loupiac Gaudiet 1988   13   £D
A pudding wine of character and richness, but best kept for the Christmas pudding in the year 2000 at which time it will mature into something even tastier and more complex.

Château Piada   12   £F
Pud plonk.

Château Septy 1986, Monbazillac   16   £C
For the price, this is a remarkable wine and quite a bargain. A bouquet of spring flowers coated with honey and
toffee which combines to produce a wine of richness that
never sinks into the cloying or heavy.

Coteaux du Layon 1982, Domaine de la
Motte   12   £D

Domaine de Lalande, Merlot Rosé 1990   13   £B
A light-hearted rosé for light-hearted occasions. Delicious
in its own way, but cannot take food.

Domaine Vincent 1990   13   £B

Ginestat Bordeaux Blanc 1989   11   £C

Mâcon Lugny 1989, Les Charmes   13   £D

Montagny 1988   11   £E

Pouilly-Fumé, Jean-Claude Châtelain 1989   10   £E

Premières Côtes de Bordeaux   13   £B
A minor dessert wine. Toffee-apple freshness makes it too
light for rich puds but fine with fresh, crisp fruits. Good
price.

St-Pourcain 1989, Domaine de Bellevue   15   £C
This marvellous bargain of a wine, which hardly anyone
has heard of, is a lovely cool, clean, appley thing with a hint
of steel all wrapped up in the right sort of refined, slightly
buttery, fruitiness. An exceptional wine with the unpre-
tentious class to pass for something altogether ritzier and
pricier – but this feature is, perhaps, only carrying on the
medieval French tradition which used to characterize any
Jacques-come-lately and his newly acquired wealth by
saying he drank this wine.

Sancerre 1989   11 £D

Sauvignon Haut-Poitou 1989   13 £C

St-Veran 1988, Cellier des Samsons   13 £D
A good, firm, clean wine.

**Tokay Pinot Gris d'Alsace 1989,
Ritzenthaler**   14 £C
Lovely fruity edge for a grape variety given to acidity.

Vilonds Muscat 1990   12 £B

Vin de Savoie, Jacquère 1990   14 £C
A revelation: a delightful blend of soft fruit and acidity
which is floral and herby, yet clean. Buy it instead of
expensive white burgundies.

Vouvray, Domaine de la Robinière 1990   12 £C

**Chardonnay, Blanc de Blancs, Le Baron de
Beaumont**   14 £C
The good baron makes a goodly wine. A bargain at under a
fiver. And as long as the good folk who drink it, thinking it
champagne, don't scrutinize the label closely, the bundle
you save at that christening or bar-mitzvah will ease your
conscience wonderfully.

GERMAN WINE – *white*

Niersteiner Dry 1989, Rheinhessen   11 £C

**Oppenheimer Herrenberg Riesling Spätlese
1988, Rheinhessen**   13 £D
Lovely aperitif. Delightfully controlled soft fruitiness.

**Oppenheimer Sackträger Silvaner Auslese
1988, Rheinhessen (half)**   10   £C
A lot of loot for a wine without the guts to spar with fruit and
dessert. So if it isn't a pud wine, what's the point of the
half-bottle?

Riesling 1988 (Waitrose) (1 litre)   11   £B

**Serriger Heiligenborn Riesling Spätlese
1983**   11   £D

ITALIAN WINE – *red*

Campo ai Sassi 1988, Rosso di Montalcino   13   £C
Deep musty Tuscan of considerable attractiveness.

**Cannonau del Parteolla 1988, Dolianova
(magnum)**   15   £D
This has to be a dinner-party talking-point: magnums are
simply more interesting than normal bottles. Who will care
that the excellent dry, fruity (and slightly spicy) wine they are
drinking hails from Sardinia and runs out at around 25p a
glass?

Carafe Red Wine (Waitrose) (1 litre)   13   £B
A highly drinkable wine for lots of pasta and lots of people.

Chianti Classico Riserva 1982, Montecastelli   12   £D
Good value if you revere older wine. It grabs the teeth like a
rotweiler – and holds on with masses of veteran fruit.

Grifi 1987, Avignonesi   13   £F
A lot of money, but a lot of wine. Elegantly earthy and fruity.

Le Pergole Torte 1985, Monte Vertine	12	£G
Monica di Sardegna 1988	11	£B
Montepulciano d'Abruzzo 1988	12	£C
Rosso Conero 1989	13	£C
Teroldego Rotaliano 1988/89	13	£C

ITALIAN WINE – *white*

Carafe White (Waitrose) (1 litre)	13	£B

Excellent value, very attractive, well-balanced dry white.

Il Marzocco, Chardonnay 1987/88	14 ('87)	£F
Avignonesi	13 ('88)	£F

1987: This is a very individual chardonnay but it is debatable whether this individuality is worth over £9. It has to be highly marked because it is stylish, clear and fresh, with an almost exotic Italian spiciness to the typical chardonnay aroma and taste.

1988: Lovely structure. A lot of dosh.

Naragus di Cagliari 1989	14	£B

One of the best white wines available at the price – clean as a whistle with a lovely hint of melon ripeness under the citric freshness.

Orvieto Classico Secco 1989, Cardeto	13	£C

As good an orvieto as you'll get.

Santa Cristina Chardonnay 1989, Zenato   14 £D
Lovely aperitif chardonnay with a delicious acid/fruit
aroma.

Soave Classico 1989, Vigneto Colombara,
Zenato   14 £C
Oh, the delicate balance this wine-maker has! – elegant,
fruity yet dry, lemon and melons, edgily rich. Delicious.

Tocai di San Martino della Battaglia 1989,
Zenato   14 £C
Beautifully constructed fruit and acid balance.

NEW ZEALAND WINE – *red*

Cook's Cabernet Sauvignon 1987, Hawkes
Bay   11 £C

NEW ZEALAND WINE – *white*

Cook's Chardonnay 1989   12 £C

Cook's Sauvignon Blanc 1989   14 £C
Try this excellent sauvignon. It's not as steely as some, but
the fruit is nicely *sotto voce* – not screaming at you like many
New World sauvignons.

PORTUGUESE WINE – *red*

Bairrada Reserva 1987, Domaine Ferraz 14 £B
Outstanding value for a fruity wine of such versatility: it
can be savoured by itself (light enough), accompany main
courses (its open, fruity style is good with food), and it has
enough acidity to cope with cheeses.

Pasmados 1985 13 £C

Tinto da Anfora 1987 15 £C
A luscious, dry, woody wine with gusto and zip. It'll put a
bomb under any food you eat with it – even rice crispies.

SPANISH WINE – *red*

Almirante de Castilla 1986, Castilla la Vieja 14 £C
None of the vanilla you get from rioja – much more elegant
than that. Not a huge bouquet for such wood-aged fruit,
but plenty of interesting flavour. Excellent with roast foods
and for dinner parties.

Castillo de Liria Valencia 15 £A
Superb value. A simple, soft, fruity wine of no great complexity but toothsome drinkability. Ripe blackcurrant on
the nose, cherries on the palate and a mix of the two in the
throat.

Cosme Palacio Rioja 1987 15 £C
A big, woody wine laced with vanilla, fruit and raisins,
which makes an excellent complement to roasts.

Don Hugo	13	£B
Gran Condal Rioja Reserva 1984	11	£C
Viña Alberdi Rioja 1986	12	£D

SPANISH WINE – *white*

Castillo de Liria Valencia (1.5 litres) 14 £A
Smashing bargain pudding wine to set the taste-buds racing.

Conde de Caralt 1989 13 £B
Dry, elegant, very good value – like a Peter Ustinov anecdote.

Cune Rioja Blanco Seco Reserva 1985 10 £D

USA WINE – *red*

Barrow Green Pinot Noir 1987, California 15 £E
A little beauty – brimming with vegetation and calm fruit. Like a good volnay and excellent value at the price.

Cartlidge & Browne, Zinfadel 1989 15 £C
What a find! Lovely, zingy, zesty stuff which just flows down the throat and screams with fruitiness all through the descent. Stylish, approachable, gorgeous. Great value and terrific at disturbing the equilibrium of wine snobs at dinner who will shudder at the word zinfadel (California's native grape, though rumoured to emanate, under the

name primitivo, from Italy) but then gasp with pleasure as
they drink the wine.

Mountain View Pinot Noir 1988	12	£C

Wente Cabernet Sauvignon 1985	11	£D

If this rich wine was £2.25 we'd all say 'Great stuff', but at
this price you have to despair at the wine's lack of integration and genuine complexity. It is rather like a Hollywood
film set or a Hollywood smile; there isn't much depth
beneath the surface.

USA WINE – *white*

Château St-Michelle Fumé Blanc 1986	10	£C

St-Andrew's Vineyard Chardonnay 1987, Napa	12	£E

Wagner Barrel Fermented Seyvel Blanc 1987	15	£D

Complexity, freshness and fullness in a most unusual yet
appealing combination. A very good wine. Really outstanding with all fish dishes from stuffed mussels to Chinese
baked sole with ginger.

YUGOSLAVIAN WINE – *red*

Milion Merlot 1986	14	£A

Soft, velvety plonk of attractive fruitiness and style at a
give-away price.

Milion Pinot Noir 1986   13   £A
This is a spicy little blighter with an engaging disposition.
If you're smart before the queues form, you'll buy several
cases of it.

SPARKLING WINE/CHAMPAGNE

Angas Brut Rosé (Australian)   12   £C
Good stuff at heart. And at under a fiver, a good thing to
take to formal dinner parties.

Blanquette de Limoux Brut (Waitrose)   11   £D

Cava Cristal Brut Castellblanch, Spain   11   £D

Crémant de Bourgogne Blanc Lugny   14   £D
Excellent dry, yet fruitily rounded, sparkling wine to be
preferred to many, many champagnes.

Crémant de Bourgogne, Brut Rosé, Lugny   12   £D
A mature, sparkling alternative to champagne.

**Extra Dry Non-Vintage Champagne
(Waitrose)**   12   £F

**Extra Dry Rosé Non-Vintage Champagne
(Waitrose)**   12   £F

**Extra Dry Vintage Champagne 1983
(Waitrose)**   17   £G
An absolutely glorious light champagne of perfumed
elegance and beauty – it celebrates itself. Quite delicious –
a bubbly of such forward and forthright charm that even
novices say, 'My word, this is something special, isn't it?' I

think it has to do with hollyhocks – how did they charm their faintly aromatic way into the wine?

Le Baron de Beaumont 13 £C
Sounds very grand, after one of Emma Bovary's unnamed aristocratic lovers *peut-être*. In glass, it is a simple but excellent lemony aperitif.

Moscato d'Asti 1990, Michele Chiarlo 14 £C
This is absolutely the dessert wine I shall serve for my birthday lunch. Sparkling creamy fruits, lemons and honey, soft like padded velvet. Lush stuff but *not* like a sauternes or a monbazillac. So be warned. The taste is an acquired one.

Saumur (Waitrose) 14 £D
Chewy little number of some distinction.

Valdo Pinot Chardonnay Brut (Italian) 12 £C